Engraved by J C Buttre

R. Hoyt

SKETCHES

OF

LIFE AND LANDSCAPE.

BY

REV. RALPH HOYT.

NEW EDITION—ENLARGED.

New-York:
STANFORD & DELISSER,
508 BROADWAY.
1858.

TO

EVERT A. DUYCKINCK, ESQ.,

THE AUTHOR'S FIRST REVIEWER, AND PRESENT FRIEND,

These Sketches

Are Inscribed, with much respect.

R. H.

New-York.

CONTENTS.

HOYT'S POEMS.

EXTRACTS FROM CRITICISMS OF THE PRESS.

"Life and Landscape, in which peaceful beauty prevails, and the sunshine of the heart is diffused over all objects."—ROCHESTER AM.

"May his poems be thumbed, re-read, and worn out in innumerable editions."—LITERARY WORLD.

It is a pleasure indeed to peruse such an author."—PHIL. POST.

"Replete with grace, delicacy, and beauty."—N. Y. COUR. & ENQ.

"Splendid music from the very heart strings."—MORNING NEWS.

"These are charming poems, full of chaste beauty."—EVENING POST.

"These effusions stamp the author as one of Nature's bards."—TRIBUNE

"We highly commend his works to all lovers of true poetry."—MIRROR.

"They will every year gain a wider celebrity, until they are known and admired wherever our language is spoken."—PHIL. BANNER.

"A natural, healthy, life-like glow, which delights while it interests the reader."—HARTFORD CALENDAR.

"A collection of some very sweet poems.—HARTFORD COURANT.

"The whole poem is a gem of the first water."—SPRINGFIELD GAZ

"We commend the poem to all lovers of English poetry.—BOSTON PAPER

"Many hearts may be touched by such strains,—all may be made better."—NEWARK ADVERTISER

"Marked by good sense, correct feeling, and a judicious taste"—CHARLESTON PATRIOT

NOTICES OF THE PRESS.

SKETCHES OF LIFE AND LANDSCAPE.—This is a delightful little book, musical as the monutain rill, dreamy as the breath of a summer evening. Mr. HOYT is a poet, and we are sure the author of such sweet poems cannot be a straight-laced sectarian. There is too much bouyancy and life, too much naturalness about him for that. He must see God in everything—see him in the clouds and in the manifold life that covers the earth—hear him in the winds and in the babbling brook, and inhale his spirit with the fresh mountain air. He can never be alone, nor tolerate aught but the natural freedom of soul which God breathed into it at its creation. This is what the spirit of this little volume says to us about Mr. Hoyt. Personally we know him not, and although Fame has borne his name to our ears, we know nothing of his peculiar beliefs and tenets. We hope, therefore, he is as good as his book, the profits of ten thousand copies of which the publishers have generously consented to give the author in aid of rebuilding the Good Shepherd Free Church, of which he is Rector, and which was destroyed by the tornado of the 21st of June last. Surely here is a way presented for giving for a religious purpose, and getting the worth of your money down. "The last Vendue," the poem that concludes the volume, is a prophetic sermon worth the price of the book.—N. Y. DISPATCH.

SKETCHES OF LIFE AND LANDSCAPE, by Rev. Ralph Hoyt. Mr. Hoyt is the Rector of the Church of the Good Shepherd, a free Episcopal Church in the upper part of the city of New York, which was entirely destroyed by a tornado, on the 21st of June last. Efforts are making to obtain funds for rebuilding it. To aid in that purpose Mr. Hoyt has collected this series of his poetical sketches, and Messrs. Stanford & Delisser publish them—the profits to be devoted to the fund. Some of them are characterized by great beauty of thought and expression. One lyric, "The World for Sale," has "gone the rounds" of the press, and been cut out and pasted into numberless scrap-books. Others have appeared in magazines, but most of them are new to the public.—ALBANY EVENING JOURNAL.

THE

TRUE LIFE;

A REVERIE:

IN THREE CANTOS.

I.

On dusky wing now night comes gently down;
  Dissolves the landscape in a vapory gray;
The monarch hills resign their sunset crown,
  Slow droop the eyelids of the drowsy day;
All weary life, and every heart oppressed,
  In soothing slumber now may sink to rest:
Save, I must vigil while all nature sleeps;
  Not self-devoted, but ordained to be
A poor way-farer o'er life's rugged steeps,
  Its sternest aspects fated still to see,
To taste its bitter draughts at many a brim,
  And chant withal earth's earnest, awful hymn

TRUE LIFE.

Thou that hast tuned my reed, if tuned it be,
  If this high prayer to such low dust belong,
Ineffable Inspirer! speak to me,
  That I sing not an inharmonious song.
Speak to me, trembling in thy glory's blaze,
  That chanting Life, withal I chant thy praise.
This earth-strung harp but teaches me to weep,
  Furrows my aching brow before its time;
O! give me now the lyre that I shall sweep
  Upon the hills of yon celestial clime:
God! make my spirit like a surging sea,
  Rolling its thundering anthems up to Thee!

Such scope I covet—fitly to adore!
  Such scope, the import of my theme to scan;
Ocean of Life! no swimmer finds a shore;
  Unfathomable mystery of Man!
So vast, so various, whence, or whither, all
  Shrouded in secrecy as with a pall!
Dread dissonance of earth! each life a note
  Swelling the mighty uproar tempest high;
Harmonious voices few, and too remote
  To temper the wild clamor of the sky;
O! for a plunge that ocean to explore!
  O! for a wing that chaos to outsoar!

TRUE LIFE

Give me to love my fellow, and in love,
  If with none other grace, to chant my strain,
Sweet key-note of soft cadences above,
  Sole star of solace in life's night of pain,
Chief gem of eden, fractured in that fall
  That ruined two fond hearts, and tarnished all!
Redeemer! be thy kindly spirit mine;
  That pearl of paradise to me restore,
Pure, fervent, fearless, lasting love, divine,
  Profound as ocean, broad as sea and shore.
While Man I sing, free, subject, and supreme,
  O! for a soul as ample as the theme!

Sad prelude I have sung, by Sorrow led
  Along the mournful shades that own her sway,
Where, by a stream that weeping eyes have shed,
  Low chanted I my melancholy lay,
In pensive concord with the sootheless wail
  Of sighing wanderers in that lonely vale.
Ah, chide not those whose wo is hard to bear,
  The heart must hover where its treasures sleep,
I saw the great, the wise, the gifted there,
  With humbler multitudes compelled to weep;
No penury, no wealth commands relief,
  No serf, no sovereign in the realms of grief!

TRUE LIFE.

Equality of wo! a form there sate,
  With regal diadem upon his brow,
But all the glory of imperial state
  Could not console that aching bosom now;
Death in his palace a dread summons spoke,
  And the stout heart of the proud monarch broke!
Unheeding such high presence, the bereaved
  Of lowlier name, despondingly around,
In silent anguish, or sad accents grieved,
  Or sternly smiled in agony profound;
So equal poor humanity appears
  In the humiliating vale of tears!

Stern lesson!—yet much profit to the soul:
  Good to be taught the nothingness of pride;
To free the spirit from earth's strong control,
  And on the sea of sorrow heavenward glide.
Humility! the burthened heart's release;
  Who enters that low portal findeth peace.
Not fair Avoca's deep sequestered dell
  Such sweet serenity and rest bestows;
Nor winding Arno's bowery banks can tell
  The weary traveller of such repose
As soothes the soul in that dim shadowy glen,
  Where mighty monarchs own themselves but men.

TRUE LIFE.

Hears now my loitering muse a stern demand;
  Why thus so long these dreary shades among?
Sad dirges sighing of the spirit-land;
  Humanity's grand lyric all unsung.
Arise, and with heroic strength be strong,
  And chime thy numbers in a worthier song!
Vain importunity, and counsel vain;
  Not mine to follow fancy's airy flight;
Earth's faithful annals must record its pain:
  Yet, oft the sun may gild the storm with light;
And hope, that makes the gloom of sorrow glow,
  On showering tears may paint life's brightest bow.

As some poor mariner adrift at sea,
  When ruthless storms have driven his bark a-wreck.
Climbing his riven mast in agony,
  The sole survivor of a crowded deck,
Sees, as he clambers upward, sad and slow,
  The dark horizon widening on his wo;
So, as I climb my splintered spar of life,
  The dreary desolation still expands;
Float by, betokening the mighty strife,
  Rude fragments from all ages and all lands;
And mournful voices answer to my soul,
  As far along the roaring surge they roll.

TRUE LIFE.

Each billow wears some diadem unclaimed,
  Or sceptre wrested from some regal hand;
Brave palaces, and castles, all unnamed,
  Yet once the glory of some mighty land;
The costliest baubles of a royal dream,
  Gone like a leaf upon a rushing stream.
There, rushing headlong, with portentous speed.
  With faded banners and strange tokens dight,
Its destiny fulfilling as decreed,
  Its crescent waning into utter night,
Dismembered, shrouded in a rayless gloom,
  The Prophet's empire hurries to its doom!

There, gone forever, o'er the heaving deep
  A mighty fabric plunges on amain,
Stern warrior ghosts a bootless vigil keep,
  In sanguine fields o'er ghastly heaps of slain;
That realm where wide the conqueror's eagles flew,
  Gone with the battle-smoke of Waterloo!
How humbled haughtiness, how calmed all rage:
  Helmet, and lance, and shield, and brazen mail,
There fill for chivalry its final page,
  As down the current gloomily they sail,
The same irrevocable doom to read,
  With Goth, and Roman, Hebrew, Greek, and Mede!

TRUE LIFE.

Old Nineveh, of great Aturian Phul,
Ecbat'na, Babylon, and Tyre remote,
Menuf, and Meroe, that in the dull
Far-distant verge of mythic ages float,
Careering still upon their fated way,
And, mote by mote, still crumbling in decay.
Great shrines of Phtha, and hundred-gated walls,
The pillared temples where old bactrians knelt,
The chiseled marble of imperial halls,
Where Pharoes, Ptolemies, and Cesars dwelt,
Strong fanes of Iuve piled to meet the sky,
Deep in the dust of perished empires lie.

There swoops in awful solitude sublime,
The shattered remnant of the elder world,
Like some primeval orb, unknown to time,
Through the wild realm of chaos helmless hurled:
On, on, forever! rushing o'er the wave,
A rebel skeleton denied a grave!
Dark, silent, desolate, an outcast globe
Blasted beneath the sin-abhorring frown;
Shorn of the sunbeam, and the verdant robe,
In an unbounded deluge still to drown!
Imponderable ruin! can it be
The morning stars sang sweetly once, for thee!

TRUE LIFE.

Dread Shape! In terror though constrained I gaze,
  The shadows of old ages roll away;
The Past is present, and the first of days
  Pours brightly down its new-created ray;
Dim, mystic visions aggregate apace,
  And primal earth stands out august in space!
How wonderful! JEHOVAH deigned to will,
  And this Creation with obedient awe
Came booming forth the mandate to fulfil;
  From darkness, glory; from disorder, law.
So pure, so beautiful, so formed for love,
  It might allure the angels from above!

I can no more! My struggling pulse beats high,
  Oppressive thought o'erwhelms my weary sense,
Absorbed in too much grief, I cannot sigh,
  Nor vent the agony that, too intense
To flow in liquid anguish, doth corrode,
  And canker where it hath its seared abode.
Then hush, my lyre; my mournful muse, adieu!
  Day breaks and calls me to its toilsome din;
Farewell ye mighty visions! but for you,
  Spirits of all my dead, too deep within
My soul's shut sanctuary ye abide,
  To be submerged in life's oblivious tide.

THE

TRUE LIFE;

A REVERIE.

II.

How changeful and how fleet the things of earth:
  But yester' the fair season of sweet flowers,
Breathing its odorous beauties into birth,
  With jessamine and roses twined the bowers;
But soon that time of bud and bloom was o'er,
  And summer glowed, where spring had smiled before:
Summer! gay, golden summer! Lo, the fields,
  Flushed with the wealth that Industry hath won;
Blithely the swain his sweeping sickle wields,
  And binds his heavy sheaves. September's sun
Tinges the clusters on the bending bough,
  And autumn holds a brief dominion now.

TRUE LIFE.

And now 'tis winter! so the moments roll
That wear out life in fanciful disguise,
And show full oft a winter in the soul,
Blight on its blossoms, gloom upon its skies;
The cherished buds of hope unblown depart,
And strew their leaves all withered on the heart.
Nor Flora's beauty, nor her sweet perfume,
O'er hills, and vales, and woodlands, can restore
The blighted tree of Life its eden bloom;
It cannot see the sun it saw before,
It cannot the decaying stem renew,
Dead, in the wintry garden where it grew!

Serenest spirit of the hallowed lyre,
Sweet soother of all sorrow, come to me;
My burdened thought with utterance inspire:
Sad harp of mine, thy saddest minstrelsie,
I here would fling upon the chilling wind,
Chanting unto the dead! Ah, how we bind
The memory of each departed joy
Close to our bleeding bosoms, till we feel
The past our only good, the earth a toy
With all its present charms. O let me steal
From the mad whirl of life, and pour my breath,
My heart, my soul, upon the ear of death!

TRUE LIFE.

Long years have sped since first I learned to sigh
Upon some dear Patroclus' funeral pyre;
Since sorrow found a channel in mine eye,
And for a buried brother, sister, sire,
Gushed out in bitter torrents, till this heart,
Drained to its depths, no more can feel the smart,
That still unsoothed hath sole dominion there;
The busy dream of life but paints it o'er
With evanescent hues as brief as fair;
The melancholy groundwork, as before,
Stands out unsoftened, unrelieved by time,
Drinks up my spirit, saps my early prime.

'Tis midnight now. Upon the latest guest,
The weary door hath made its final close,
And one sweet hour of deep, oblivious rest,
Shall yield my soul luxurious repose—
My soul, o'erworn on life's tumultuous sea,
And sighing for that stream where peacefully
The pillowed mariners unconscious glide,
Soothed in a dreamless, care-dispelling sleep:
O! let me launch upon that lethean tide,
Thought shall be rocked a-slumber, and a deep,
Deep plunge of memory beneath its wave
Shall leave my spirit quiet as the grave.

TRUE LIFE.

Illusive hope; as soon yon gem of night,
  Soft peering through my casement from on high,
Shall cease its vigilings and quench its light,
  Tired of its toilsome errands up the sky;
While none but He who lighted up its ray,
  May bid that little twinkler pass away.
Star of my Life! etherial mystic flame,
  Kindled in heaven, yet deigned to me on earth,
Know thou thy destiny is e'en the same:
  Burn till He gives thee rest, who gave thee birth:
From thought no solitude can set thee free,
  The world shut out, shuts in thyself to thee.

That spark aloft at midnight brighter glows,
  In silence gleams in its sublimest power;
So thou, my soul, while grief around thee throws
  Its gloomy curtain, let it be the hour
Thy noblest energies to freely pour,
  Yet not to shine,—but from the earth to soar.
For what is earth, that spirit e'er should dwell
  E'en in its sweetest eden? Let this dust
Cling to its fading kindred,—it is well:
  The soul hath riches where there is no rust,
Afar, in heaven, a paradisial grot,
  Where joy's perfection is, and sorrow cometh not.

TRUE LIFE.

Now let me call up from the misty past,
  The venerable one 'twas mine to love
Till manhood's years upon my brow had cast
  Their boding shadows ;—he is now above,
Nor would I bring him thence,—but oh, to greet
  That reverend form once more, how sweet, how sweet.
Father! I need not haunt thy resting place,
  Nor send my thoughts to seek among the blest,
Thy care-worn countenance again to trace:
  Here lives thy image in this burning breast!
And here it still shall glow, nor ever fade,
  Till low beside thee thy lone child is laid.

I wot again a flower in life's bright morn,
  The solace, and the hope, and ay, the pride
Of its fond, fostering stem,—that flower was torn
  By a rude tempest from its parent's side:
Where are its beauties now?—go ask the tomb:
  That rosy child,—where now its living bloom?
I trode his father's hall, and used to hear
  His little step light tripping in its glee,
But now I hear it not,—and lo, a tear
  Springs in that eye so gladsome wont to be:
Death hath shed mildew on its dearest joy,
  Borne to the silent world that prattling boy.

Yet can it be that he no more shall come?
  See, here are all his pastime toys arranged
As though this moment he had left his home,
  The recreative for the school-hour changed.
There stands his kite against the chamber wall,
  There hangs his garden hat, there lies his ball,
And here, with scientific skill disposed,
  His tiny cabinet is ope to view;
Would he have left the little door unclosed,
  Were he to sojourn a long year or two?
Ah! now upon the dusty shelves I see
  The sad solution,—death—eternity!

And where is Ida? Answer ye sweet flowers
  Here clustering in the path she loved to tread;
Oft from her hand ye drank the mimic showers;
  Now whither hath the gentle Ida fled?
Fair stream, along whose margin oft she strayed,
  Where wanders now the lovely, lonely maid?
The lover's bosom heaves the frequent sigh,
  The hearts of dear companions inly weep,
The varying seasons drearily roll by,
  Yet Ida seems in some enchanted sleep.
Sweet maiden, why so long in slumber bound?
  Ah! mark yon willow!—Ask the turfy ground!

TRUE LIFE

O dream of time!—Yet good to ponder o'er
  The strange vicissitudes of this low sphere;
To muse how swiftly from its rock-bound shore
  Life's voyagers set sail and disappear:
How phantom-like the generations pass,
  Confessing as they fly, all flesh is grass.
Hope draws the outline, let the honest hand
  Of truth fill up the picture, till we see
Life's lights and shades as they are wont to stand,
  On the broad canvass of reality.
Reality, yet strangely frail as fair,
  Substantial landscape, painted on the air.

Mysterious!—It is the hallowed time
  When spirits are abroad; and, while I gaze,
My buried bosom ones assume their prime,
  And greet me with the smiles of other days;
And whom I love on earth, a cherished few,
  Press with the visioned dead upon my view.
From guileless infancy, to silvered age,
  They crowd to make the catalogue complete,
As from my heart's imperishable page,
  Their deep engraven names my thoughts repeat:
Be these my pencil's theme, while I portray
  Life's budding, blooming, bearing, and decay.

TRUE LIFE.

Come, my Letitia,—mine by that strange tie
  Which makes us ever love the artless soul;
Now let me look into that lustrous eye,
  And trace the course thy coming years shall roll:
Th' original for life's first picture be,
  The early stem before the towering tree.
Ha! there's a change upon that tiny cheek:
  Smile on! not I thy joy would ever mar,
Though mournfully it makes the past to speak,
  And sorrow's heavy step recalls afar:
Smile on, and claim my pencil's brightest hues,
  Life's rainbow tints, to look upon, and lose.

Oh, would I were, my cherub child, like thee,
  So newly from the skies, that earth hath gained
No inlet for its deep impurity:
  Oh, would I were like thee, so soul-unstained!
Sweet Innocence! my thought, my hand be still;
  The holy theme demands an angel's skill.
Hope of thy mother, could her mandate stay
  The hours that bear thee from a sinless heart,
Full amply would thy lessened pangs repay
  The love that dared to keep thee as thou art.
But time's swift tide will ne'er forbear to flow,
  The little bark must on, the bud must blow.

THE

TRUE LIFE;

A REVERIE.

III.

LIFE'S germ from heaven, though on earth the bloom,
And seems the flower with full perfection blest;
But ah, there's poison in its sweet perfume,
And spots appear within its snowy breast.
How could I weep in sootheless, ceaseless grief,
That life so soon is sere and yellow leaf.
Perfidious heart; so subtle, so debased;
But for the bitterness in it that springs,
The tearful history were soon erased,
And earth-born man would soar on seraph wings.
Ah, heart, thou need'st the re-creating sway
Of Him who is the Life, the Truth, the Way.

TRUE LIFE.

I see the awful vision of all time;
  All life, since man became a living soul;
All change, since woman taught him love; and crime,
  And death's dark wave began o'er earth to roll:
Stupendous pomp! far reaching to that night
  Ere stars were kindled, or the sun gave light.
Swayed as eternal symphonies impel,
  Chord answering chord, mysterious harps I hear,
And myriad voices still the anthem swell,
  Pouring grand harmonies from sphere to sphere;
Chanting historic, the great psalm of earth,
  Since chaos labored with its mighty birth.

Man, the epitome! Still chiefly he
  The mighty argument of that high song;
Of His omnipotence who bade him be,
  Sublimest miracle of all the throng
That at his mandate from the nought of space
  Came forth, substantial majesty and grace.
Materiality, and essence, each
  Its full perfection in his form to find:
A universe articulate in his speech;
  All spirit-greatness imaged in his mind.
Harp on forever, all ye bards above;
  Man still your theme, and man-creating love!

Yet must you mourn, ye minstrels of the sky;
Through all your strains still sweeps a note of woe,
As myriad hearts were breaking in one sigh;
Now in profoundest octaves moaning low;
Up the careering scale now frantic flies,
Shrieks its sad tale in heaven, and wailing dies.
Me now instruct, that justly I discourse
Those joys and sorrows, your immortal themes;
Reveal of each the annals and the source;
And as I, listening, muse along the streams,
And o'er the mountains, all my thoughts inspire
Till your high burden thrill my lowly lyre.

'Tis evening now, and all the stars again,
Like pensive spirits, look lamenting down;
A sister orb woe-smitten! and a stain,
How deep and lasting, on its old renown.
What envious hand so impiously could dare,
To mar so mournfully a world so fair.
Would I might speak to them; my soul would know
From those high witnesses, so pure and true,
Whence came, and why, the desolating blow
Could leave such deserts where such edens grew;
Could doom to perish an immortal race,
And earth itself to fail and have no place.

TRUE LIFE.

Speak, stars, ye nightly mourners; and no more
  In mute amazement wait the coming hour
That shall earth's wasted excellence restore,
  And give man back his innocence and power,
Too long your silent sorrow; sootheless grief
  May quench your glory, yet bring no relief.
Known your sad secret; mark the fearful word
  Rebellion! traced on every human brow;
And oft in scathing tempests hath been heard
  The tale that moves your deep compassion now.
O, to my call, ye weeping worlds, reply;
  Man and his home in ruin! tell me why!

Great Volume of the Word; behold, in thee
  The dark enigma is resolved and clear;
But lo, the eye of nature cannot see,
  And ah, the ear too heavy, cannot hear.
His paradise how long with wo o'erspread;
  And the immortal dweller, outcast, dead!
Dead; yet infatuated not to know
  Essential vigor, beauty, truth, and love
Fled when he dealt the self-destroying blow,
  And lost the Life that cometh from above.
O, Word Almighty, the dread bondage break;
  Awake the sleeper, bid the dead awake!

TRUE LIFE.

Companion mine, along this devious page
  Let me a tale to thee discourse awhile,
May haply much thy curious ear engage,
  And this brief hour right worthily beguile;
Yet, as the chronicle unfolds to view,
  Though fancy's record, deem the burden true.
In sooth, my soul is fain to seek repose,
  And would to thee its lore of years impart;
The meditative gatherings disclose,
  That miser memory garners in the heart;
A tale of death, pride, passion, riches, fame,
  And virtue tried in love's intensest flame.

In a sweet vale amid a desert waste,
  There dwelt a maiden radiant as light;
As a pure angel delicate and chaste;
  No lovelier form e'er greeted mortal sight;
Nor lived she but to bless, and wide to show
  The living joys that truth and love bestow.
At every fount of knowledge drank she deep;
  Not erudition's sages so profound;
Of things divine could scale the cloudy steep,
  And all the depths of faith and reason sound;
Yet ever meek, no one desire she knew,
  Save still to be all heavenly and true.

TRUE LIFE.

These peerless charms and all-surpassing grace,
  That humble vale might not unknown retain;
A world were blest to look upon that face,
  And contemplate a heart that knew no stain.
From hill to hill wide flew the wondrous tale,
  So bright a gem in such a lowly vale!
Came one and knelt adoring at her shrine;
  And, sooth, a great and seemly suitor he;
Could she his prayer and plighted troth decline?
  Ah, who can know a maiden's mind, perdie!
Not all unmoved his suppliance she heard,
  Yet gave no hope, save only 'hope deferred.'

Ah, gentle fair, why thus my suit disdain,
  Cried he, reproachful, with offended pride:
A nobler name in story must I gain;
  What task performed shall win thee for my bride?
Though years attest my studious toil for thee,
  Yet say what more to do; what more to be.
Then she, all-pitying, raised a tearful eye,
  And owned the fond emotion of her breast,
But thoughtful, drew a deep deploring sigh,
  And a strange, startling answer thus expressed;
O, noble youth, though earth's best gifts are shed
  Around and on thee, thou, alas, art dead!

TRUE LIFE

As starts a dreamer when some hideous shape
The slumbering sense with sudden terror thrills;
So he, with shuddering soul, would fain escape
Back to the refuge of his native hills.
But still transfixed he stood, in mute dismay,
Till all like some dread vision passed away.
Again ere long to conscious thought returned,
He sighed the import of those words to know;
Dead! while his bosom with such ardor burned;
Love, reason, and ambition all a-glow;
Yet oh, that word, with such dark meaning fraught;
And that sweet spirit; could they be for nought?

The maiden's bower again he trembling sought,
And prayed a lover's pure impassioned prayer;
O, might he at her feet the truth be taught;
Or would she but vouchsafe to tell him where,
Where might he terminate the doubtful strife;
And find, if he were dead, the soul's true life.
O, sweet to see how she inclined the ear;
How soon disclosed the "the true and living way;"
And ah, how brake his heart the brimming tear
That bade him never from her love to stray,
As forth, elate, with hastening step she trode,
And showed a temple—Truth's august abode.

Now, onward thou, she cried, the mountain climb,
And press for yonder porch with steadfast heart;
There enter, and the wisdom of old-time
Its prophet-voices shall to thee impart;
Obey, and lo, thou shalt to life arise,
And this, my long-sought hand shall be thy prize.
Then thitherward a wistful look he cast,
Bending his step within a narrow way;
And on his joyous pilgrimage he passed,
Still wending onward all the weary day,
'Till at the portal pausing, lowly there
He knelt and breathed a penitential prayer.

O, Fount of Life! in thy blest courts how free
The sacramental stream all-cleansing flows,
When the benighted wanderer bends the knee,
And o'er his head the mystic waters close.
Baptismal Jordan! and the Spirit-Dove!
Life, Reconciliation, Peace, and Love!
So knew the pilgrim as the ghostly shower
From holy hands descended on his head.
Regenerated! By redeeming power
Awaked from sleep; arisen from the dead!
How flashed the light! What rapture thrilled the youth;
There, and forever his, were LIFE and TRUTH.

JULIA.

JULIA.—Chester—Julia's Home—Departure—Grief for Absence—October Scenes—The River Bronx—The Poet Drake—Traveller at the Cottage—The Welcome—Rustic Evening Pastimes—The Stranger and Julia—Recollections—Early Pledge—Rambles—Nutting—Apple Gathering—Threshing—Rejection—Disclosure—Recognition—Delight in the Cottage—Conclusion.

JULIA.

As sudden sunshine gilds a murky sky,
  Or moonbeams tip the raven wings of night,
That happy word illumined Julia's eye,
  Made all the clouds of her dark sorrow bright,
And filled the cottage with a new delight

JULIA,

AN AUTUMNAL TALE.

WHERE rural Chester spreads in hill and plain,
And rippling Bronx pursues its peaceful way,
Just as you turn within a winding lane,
Skirting the border of a little bay,
There stands a cottage ivied-o'er and gray.

The home of JULIA's joyous spring of life;
Ere the sweet blossom ripened into love,
Ere she had known the autumn of its strife,
The cold rude blasts that pierce the gentle Dove,
And warn its wing to calmer climes above.

Alas, there came a change upon her heart,
A hopeless sorrow like an April blight:
For other lands she saw her swain depart;
And swift departed then each gay delight,
Spring became Winter,—Morning turned to night!

Still climbed the wood-bine by the cottage door,
Still sang the robin sweetly to his mate,
Still strove parental fondness as before,
But JULIA's grief still knew but one dark date,
And flower and song and love came all too late.

It was OCTOBER,—sadly wailed the breeze,
As o'er the hill and through the wood it sped;
The fruit was gathered from thè sapless trees,
A frosty veil the meadows overspread,
And all the groves were withering or dead.

The harvest fields of all their treasures shorn
Betrayed again the rude unseemly ground;
Where grew the bending wheat, the towering corn,
But stubble now, and leafless stalks were found,
Furrow, and ridge, the fading landscape round.

Fair CHESTER seemed like some desponding maid,
The scene so sad beneath the autumn sky;
Her summer sun to rival climates strayed,
Her dewy pearls ungathered left to lie,
And limpid Bronx in grief to murmur by.

JULIA.

(Ah, gentle stream, glide on in ceaseless wo,
  While by thy margin sleeps thy plaintive bard,
Sweet minstrel Drake! Ye autumn winds sing low!
  Ye seasons all, leave that green slope unmarred
Where yon lone willows his dear ashes guard.)

There came a stranger to the gate one eve,
  And craved in gentle words to be a guest;
Might that sweet cot his weariness relieve,
  Now day so far was drooping down the west;
A pilgrim's blessing on the roof should rest

All welcome ever to that kindly hearth;
  None sought its plenty or its peace in vain;
Though pensive JULIA knew no more of mirth,
  Yet none abiding there might know her pain,
Did in her heart such holy calmness reign.

Came hastening on the chill autumnal night,
  With rustic pastime and its guiltless glee,
The floor was stainless, and the fire was bright,
  The nuts were cracking upon every knee,
And new-made cider flowed most sweet and free.

JULIA.

High rose the mirth as from the embers flew
 The roasting chesnut with a sudden start,
For blushing John, or Jane, an omen true
 Of love's sly passion glowing in the heart,
And Hymen's speedy aid with his sweet art.

The stranger's heart was moved by JULIA's grace
 And oft he gazed, as bound by beauty's spell,
Upon her faultless form and winning face,
 And as he felt the pure emotion swell
He longed the secret of his love to tell.

Nor he unworthy such a maid to win;
 Of noble aspect, manly, yet serene;
No foul deceiver, stained with reckless sin;
 In sportive group upon the village green,
He were a goodly king, and she a queen.

With gentle accents soon, and whispering low,
 Besought he JULIA for a hopeful smile;
But ah, his suit still added to her wo—
 Her mournful thoughts were far away the while,
And loving words might not her heart beguile.

JULIA.

Ah! stranger said she sweetly, one I knew
  Who wooed and won this simple heart of mine,
And to his image still it must be true,
  Though weary seasons it may yet repine,
Till life's last sun of hope in death decline.

'Twas autumn e'en as now when last we met,
  And seven long years their dreary course have run,
Since here we plighted, never to forget;
  That holy pledge I may recal for none;
One shares my silent love,—and only one.

I still remember how we used to rove,
  Young and light-hearted in the frosty Fall,
Far in the lonely depths of nut-wood grove,
  List'ning the squirrel's chirp, the cat-bird's call,
Hid from the world, and happier than all.

How through the rustling leaves we loved to walk,
  Our ample baskets bountifully stored,
As hand in hand we held our cheerful talk,
  And still each nook for hidden nuts explored
Proud to bear home an unexampled hoard

JULIA.

Oft through the bending orchard have I prest,
  Among the fruits in rich abundance there,
To cull for him the ripest and the best,
  The evening pastime early to prepare,
Undreaming then that love is linked with care!

When in the barn the laborers and he
  Threshed out the treasures of the ripened sheaf,
How sweet the music of his flail to me!
  But all is over,—save my helpless grief,
And life to me is now an autumn leaf!

Oh stranger, there be fairer maids than I
  Would proudly welcome such a proffered hand;
Your lordly wealth a paradise may buy,
  But vain for me the glittering, or grand;
My sootheless heart is in another land.

Said then the traveler, I knew full well
  Your wandering Youth in Oriental climes;
Oft have I heard him of sweet Chester tell,
  Repeat its tales, rehearse its rustic rhymes,
And talk of all its pleasant autumn times.

JULIA.

The ardent skies where he has sojourned long,
  Have tinged his visage with the Indian hue ;
His youthful limbs have stalwart grown and strong ;
  And scarce his voice might now be known to you ;
Yet beats his heart unalterably true !

How cruel was the storm that wrecked his bark,
  And drove him helmless o'er the raging wave ;
Above, below, and all around him dark,
  No voice to soothe him, and no hand to save,
No hope, no refuge but a billowy grave,

And when the rescue came, and bore him far
  Through widening seas to India's distant shore,
How sank in gloom his bosom's love-lit star,
  How seemed the visions of his home all o'er,
Without a promise he should see it more.

But still he lives !—and in his dreams of bliss
  His faithful Julia all his ardor claims ;
Oft has he longed for such an hour as this,
  Oft in his prayer his cherished one he names ;
Dear angel !—I am he,— your long lost James !

As sudden sunshine gilds a murky sky,
  Or moonbeams tip the raven wings of night,
That happy word illumined Julia's eye,
  Made all the clouds of her dark sorrow bright,
And filled the cottage with a new delight.

The glowing hearth grew warmer than before,
  The baking apples tumbled to and fro,
The singing kettle instant spouted o'er,
  Kate could no longer spin, nor Sally sew,
And e'en the wind seemed gladsomely to blow!

Joined all the household in a loving din;
  Fantastic shadows danced upon the wall,
Such clasping, kissing, gliding out and in!
  Such leaping, laughing, talking, one and all,
It might be deemed a romping rustic Ball!

Still rural Chester spreads in hill and plain,
  Still murmurs rippling Bronx its autumn lay,
Still stands a ruin in that winding lane,
  Skirting the border of a little bay,—
But all the dwellers there have passed away!

EDWARD BELL.

EDWARD BELL.—May Morning—Children at a Brook—Innocence—Artless Love—Scenes in May—The Chanting Stream—Odorous Air—Sunshine—Two of the Children—Attachment—Delights of the Season—Early Dawn—Glittering Dew—Plough-Boy—John and Sophy—Mill-Wheel—Wagons—Smoke at a Distance—Birds—Fountain—Woodman's Song—Teamster Whistling—Jane—Noisy Poultry—Lambs at Play—Pleasant Musing—The Catastrophe.

EDWARD BELL.

A RURAL SKETCH OF MAY.

One bright May morning there were children playing
By a brook;
There was no care upon their young hearts weighing;
No sad look:
The forests, fields, and flowers were green and gay,
That morn in May.

And they were six, those children, sweetly mated
Two and two;
Three urchins and three maidens, and they prated
As such do:
They prattled, played, and helped the birds to sing
The rosy Spring!

Full simple and all artless was the story
That each told;
But truth and innocence have still a glory
As of old;
And rudest childhood may inspire a page
For wisest age.

Oh life! why are thy early joys forsaken!
Why should time
Lull innocence to slumber, and awaken
Pride and crime!
Oh years, oh change, how swift ye bear away
Life's sinless May!

They were not whispering the shame of others:
Nor would fling
The brand of enmity among earth's brothers:
Nor the sting
Of jealous rivalry did they endure,—
For they were pure!

They loved each other, and they loved the flowers,
Streams and trees,
The vine slow creeping o'er the latticed bowers,
Buzzing bees,
The mossy cottage, and the old stone wall,—
They loved them all.

The fragrant cluster of wild roses glowing
In the dell,
Pink, woodbine, lilach, and sweet-briar blowing
By the well,
With holly-hock, like soldiery around,
Guarding the ground.

Oh, could the sordid ones of earth have listened
Each sweet word—
The heart had softened and the eye had glistened
While they heard:
Such guileless love, such gentleness were there,—
Alas, so rare!

MAY! o'er the distant wood the crow is swelling
His wild cry;
To pilfering broods in sprouting cornfields telling
Danger nigh!
Just as the ambushed farmer to the sun
Betrays his gun.

Loud chants the brook, some lovelorn myth repeating;
Shouts each boy;
E'en drifting leaves, in little eddies meeting,
Dance for joy;
The odorous air, the sky, the sun's warm ray
All make it MAY!

EDWARD BELL.

But there were two among the group that season.
Edward Bell,
And one whose name the muse with mournful reason,
Shrinks to tell—
An angel girl—the eldest that was there,
And passing fair.

They sat together where the trees o'ershaded,
And they walked
Along the margin of the stream, or waded,
Sang and talked,
And looked into each other's eyes to say—
Oh, sweet, sweet—May!

And they discoursed of all the rural pleasures
Spring imparts;
Field, garden, grove,—how full of truest treasures
For true hearts!
The sweet vicissitude—the toil—the rest,
Supremely blest!

How painted he the picture of the morning
From the dawn:
The cock's shrill trumpet earliest in warning;
The green lawn,
The rising mist, the far receding night,
The orient light!

EDWARD BELL.

The dewy glitter as the sun came peeping
O'er the hill;
The lonely willow, where the loved were sleeping,
Weeping still;
The skylark mounting with his matin lay
To meet the day.

The drowsy plough-boy to the meadow wending
For the team,
The barnyard choir their rueful concert blending
With his dream;
The laden cows slow gathering before
The dairy door.

The creaking bars that John lets down for Sophy
With her pails;
The hasty kiss he seizes as a trophy
O'er the rails;
The patient oxen yoked and ready now
To speed the plough.

The grumbling mill-wheel indolently starting,
And the corn
In rustic wagons coming and departing;
The far horn
Calling to the repast some swain remote,
With welcome note

The curling smoke some distant cot denoting
'Mid the trees :
The low bright clouds along the azure floating;
The soft breeze,
Where blooming orchards their sweet odors fling
The Spring,—the Spring!

So penciled he, that youth, with raptured feeling
Yet serene,
The guileless fountain of his heart revealing,
That fair scene:
And she, elate, delight in each blue eye,
Made sweet reply.

'Twas her's to paint the dear domestic heaven
That she knew :
The tranquil joys, from early morn till even,
Pure and true ;
The peace that seeks more oft the cottage gate
Than courtly state.

How eloquent to her each simple token
Of the time,
The day's approach,—the chains of slumber broken
The sweet chime
Of songsters warbling from the budding spray—
Hail, flowery MAY !

EDWARD BELL.

The cool ablution at the dripping fountain,
By the bower;
(A crystal treasure newly from the mountain,
Since the shower,)
The woodman's lay soft echoing on the ear,
Oh, sweet to hear!

The strain now near,—and faintly now receding
On the air;
Now heard,—now hushed again, some breeze impeding,
Yet seems there,—
The lingering cadence haunting all the sky,
Too pure to die!

But yonder whistling teamster home returning
O'er the farm,
Slow wheeling up his load of brush for burning,
Breaks the charm;
The crackling branches, and the axe' sharp fall
Out-echoing all!

And now the blazing hearth, fair Jane preparing
Her rich store:
The idle dog the clamorous poultry scaring
From the door:
The frisking colt, the two pet lambs at play;
'Tis May,—'tis May!

EDWARD BELL.

So mused that gentle pair, the time beguiling,
That bright day;
Dreamed not the joyous group, that hours so smiling
Pass away!
They prattled, played, and helped the birds to sing,
The rosy Spring!

Ah, brook and flowery bank how soon forsaken!
Ah, that time
Should lull our truth to slumber, and awaken
Pride and crime!
Oh years, oh change, how swift ye bear away
Youth's happy May!

One morn again a poor old man was straying
By the brook:
Sore seemed the sorrow on his bent form weighing,
Sad his look:
For him nor field nor flowers were green, or gay,
Though it was May.

He gazed as dreaming of some brighter morning,
Ere his wo:
He missed the fairest flower that bank adorning,
Long ago!
Five turfy mounds were there—there dead he fell!
'Twas Edward Bell!

SNOW.

SNOW.—Snow Falling—The Landscape—Martial Resemblances—Drifts and Disguises—Mystery of the Well—Pranks of the Wood-Pile, Axe, Log, the Kennel, and the Grindstone—Astonishment in the Roost—Cattle in the Barn-Yard—Delight of the Children—Domestic Worship—The Breakfast—Business of the Day—Preparations for a Sleigh-Ride—Conclusion.

SNOW.

The jocund fields would masquerade;
Fantastic scene!
Tree, shrub, and lawn, and lonely glade
Have cast their green,
And joined the revel, all arrayed
So white and clean.

SNOW,

A WINTER SKETCH.

THE blessed morn has come again;
The early gray
Taps at the slumberer's window pane,
And seems to say
Break, break from the enchanter's chain,
Away, away!

'Tis Winter, yet there is no sound
Along the air,
Of winds upon their battle-ground,
But gently there,
The snow is falling,—all around
How fair—how fair!

SNOW.

The jocund fields would masquerade;
Fantastic scene!
Tree, shrub, and lawn, and lonely glade
Have cast their green,
And joined the revel, all arrayed
So white and clean.

E'en the old posts, that hold the bars
And the old gate,
Forgetful of their wintry wars
And age sedate,
High capped, and plumed, like white hussars,
Stand there in state.

The drifts are hanging by the sill,
The eaves, the door;
The hay-stack has become a hill;
All covered o'er
The wagon, loaded for the mill
The eve before.

Maria brings the water-pan,
But where's the Well!
Like magic of a fairy tale,
Most strange to tell,
All vanished curb, and crank, and rail!
How deep it fell!

The wood-pile too is playing hide;
The axe, the log,
The kennel of that friend so tried,
(The old watch-dog,)
The grindstone standing by its side,
All now *incog*.

The bustling cock looks out aghast
From his high shed;
No spot to scratch him a repast
Up curves his head,
Starts the dull hamlet with a blast
And back to bed.

Old drowsy dobbin, at the call,
Amazed, awakes;
Out from the window of his stall
A view he takes,
While thick and faster seem to fall
The silent flakes.

The barn-yard gentry, musing, chime
Their morning moan;
Like Memnon's music of old time
That voice of stone!
So marbled they—and so sublime
Their solemn tone.

SNOW.

Good Ruth has called the younker folk
To dress below;
Full welcome was the word she spoke.
Down, down they go,
The cottage quietude is broke,—
The snow!—the snow!

Now rises from around the fire
A pleasant strain;
Ye giddy sons of mirth, retire!
And ye profane!
A hymn to the Eternal Sire
Goes up again.

The patriarchal Book divine,
Upon the knee,
Opes where the gems of Judah shine,
(Sweet minstrelsie!)
How soars each heart with each fair line
Oh God, to Thee!

Around the altar low they bend,
Devout in prayer;
As snows upon the roof descend,
So angels there
Come down that household to defend
With gentle care.

SNOW

Now sings the kettle o'er the blaze;
The buckwheat heaps;
Rare Mocha, worth an Arab's praise,
Sweet Susan steeps;
The old round stand her nod obeys,
And out it leaps.

Unerring presages declare
The banquet near;
Soon, busy appetites are there;
And disappear
The glories of the ample fare,
With thanks sincere.

Now tiny snow-birds venture nigh
From copse and spray,
(Sweet strangers! with the winter's sky
To pass away;)
And gather crumbs in full supply,
For all the day.

Let now the busy hours begin:
Out rolls the churn;
Forth hastes the farm-boy, and brings in
The brush to burn;
Sweep, shovel, scour, sew, knit, and spin,
'Till night's return.

SNOW

To delve his threshing John must hie;
  His sturdy shoe
Can all the subtle damp defy;
  How wades he through!
While dainty milkmaids, slow and shy,
  His track pursue.

Each to the hour's allotted care;
  To shell the corn;
The broken harness to repair;
  The sleigh t' adorn;
As cheerful, tranquil, frosty, fair,
  Speeds on the morn;

While mounts the eddying smoke amain
  From many a hearth,
And all the landscape rings again
  With rustic mirth;
So gladsome seems to every swain
  The SNOWY earth.

TO MARY;

A WINTER RETROSPECT.

WHEN lately, fair cousin, you sued for a dozen
  Brief lines in a song or a sonnet,
Though little you knew it, I trembled to do it,
  For thoughts of our youth came upon it;
A sad retrospection of early affection;
  The joys of our infancy's morning;
Of many warm hearted now cold or departed;
  Dark changes that came without warning.

When over the heather we journeyed together,
  Or roved in the meadow, beguiling
Our holiday hours in gathering flowers,
  While the bright summer skies were smiling,
As sister and brother were we to each other;
  As lovers whom nought could dissever,
Nor knew that that feeling was rapidly stealing
  Away like a meteor forever.

TO MARY

And while we remember, as frosty December
  Comes bristling along in his ire,
How cheated the season so out of all reason,
  Our glee by the crackling fire;
'Tis mournfully pleasant to look from the present
  Far back on those days of gladness,
But none can restore them, dark shadows are o'er them,
  And memory sinks in sadness.

Yet what is life's trouble; a fable, a bubble,
  Unreal, or soon to vanish;
A cloud on a mountain, the mist o'er a fountain,
  Which the first beam of morn will banish.
There cometh an hour of balmiest power.
  When gloom shall afar be driven,
And when we shall fleetly, yet calmly and sweetly
  Go up to our rest in heaven.

The years in their rolling thus whisper consoling;
  And deep though they leave their traces,
Disrobing the roses where beauty reposes,
  While furrows of care take their places,
Though thus they pursue us, tney shall not subdue us,
  But when through our course we have wended,
Life's stormiest billow will seem a sweet pillow,
  And all in love's ocean be ended.

WORLD-SALE.

World-Sale.—Descent of a Celestial Youth—His Birth as a Mortal—Happiness of his Childhood—Wanderings in Many Lands—Final Disappointment—Return to his Early Home—Change and Sorrow There—Longing for Heaven—Resolution to Part with Earthly Joys—The Sale—Wealth—Love—Friendship—Fame—Hope—Song—Ambition.

THE

WORLD-SALE,

A MORAL SKETCH.

THERE wandered from some mystic sphere,
 A Youth, celestial, down to earth;
So strangely fair seemed all things here,
 He e'en would crave a mortal birth:
And soon, a rosy boy, he woke,
 A dweller in some stately dome;
Soft sunbeams on his vision broke,
 And this low world became his home.

WORLD-SALE.

Ah, cheated child! Could he but know
  Sad soul of mine, what thou and I!
The bud would never wish to blow,
  The nestling never long to fly;
Perfuming the regardless air,
  High soaring into empty space;
A blossom ripening to despair,
  A flight—without a resting place!

How bright to him life's opening morn!
  No cloud to intercept a ray;
The rose had then no hidden thorn,
  The tree of life knew no decay.
How greeted oft his wondering soul
  The fairy shapes of childish joy,
As gaily on the moments stole
  And still grew up the blooming boy

How gently played the odorous air
  Among his wavy locks of gold,
His eye how bright, his cheek how fair,
  As still youth's summer days were told
Seemed each succeeding hour to tell
  Of some more rare unfolding grace;
Some swifter breeze his sail to swell,
  And press the voyager apace!

WORLD-SALE.

He roved a swain of some sweet vale,
Or climbed, a daring mountaineer;
And oft, upon the passing gale,
His merry song we used to hear;
Might none e'er mount a fleeter steed,
His glittering chariot none outvie,
Or village mart, or rural mead,
The hero he of heart and eye.

Anon a wishful glance he cast
Where storied thrones their empire hold,
And soon beyond the billowy Vast
He leaped upon the shores of old!
He sojourned long in classic halls,
At learning's feast a favored guest,
And oft within imperial walls,
He tasted all delights, save—rest!

It was a restless soul he bore,
And all unquenchable its fire;
Nor banquet, pomp, nor golden store,
Could e'er appease its high desire.
And yet would he the phantom band
So oft deceiving still pursue,
Delicious sweets in every land,
But ah, not lasting, pure or true

WORLD-SALE.

He knelt at many a gorgeous shrine;
  Reclined in love's voluptuous bowers;
Yet did his weary soul repine,
  Were listless still the lingering hours.
Then sped an argosie to bear
  The sated truant to his home,
But sorrow's sombre cloud was there,
  'Twas dark in all that stately dome.

Was rent at last life's fair disguise,
  And that Immortal taught to know
He had been wandering from the skies,
  Alas, how long—alas, how low!
Deluded,—but the dream was done;
  A conqueror,—but his banner furled;
The race was over,—he had won,—
  But found his prize—a worthless World!

Oh Earth, he sighed, and gazed afar,
  How thou encumberest my wing!
My home is yonder radiant star,
  But thither thee I cannot bring.
How have I tried thee long and well,
  But never found thy joys sincere,
Now, now my soul resolves to sell
  Thy treasures strewn around me here!

WORLD-SALE.

The flatteries I so long have stored
  In memory's casket one by one,
Must now be stricken from the hoard
  The day of tinselled joy is done!
Here go the useless jewels! see
  The golden lustre they impart!
But vain the smiles of earth for me,
  They cannot gild a broken heart!

THE WORLD FOR SALE!—Hang out the sign;
  Call every traveller here to me;
Who'll buy this brave estate of mine,
  And set me from earth's bondage free!
'Tis going!—yes I mean to fling
  The bauble from my soul away;
I'll sell it, whatsoe'er it bring;—
  The World at Auction here to-day!

It is a glorious thing to see;
  Ah, it has cheated me so sore!
It is not what it seems to be:
  For sale! It shall be mine no more.
Come, turn it o'er and view it well;
  I would not have you purchase dear;
'Tis going—going! I must sell!
  Who bids! Who'll buy the Splendid Tear!

WORLD-SALE

Here's Wealth in glittering heaps of gold,
  Who bids! but let me tell you fair,
A baser lot was never sold;
  Who'll buy the heavy heaps of care
And here, spread out in broad domain,
  A goodly landscape all may trace;
Hall, cottage, tree, field, hill and plain;
  Who'll buy himself a Burial Place!

Here's Love, the dreamy potent spell
  That beauty flings around the heart!
I know its power, alas, too well!
  'Tis going! Love and I must part!
Must part! What can I more with Love!
  All over the enchanter's reign!
Who'll buy the plumeless, dying dove,
  An hour of bliss,—an age of Pain!

And Friendship,—rarest gem of earth,
  (Who e'er hath found the jewel his ?)
Frail, fickle, false and little worth,
  Who bids for Friendship—as it is!
'Tis going—going!—Hear the call;
  Once, twice, and thrice!—'Tis very low!
'Twas once my hope, my stay, my all,
  But now the broken staff must go!

WORLD-SALE.

FAME! hold the brilliant meteor high
  How dazzling every gilded name!
Ye millions, now's the time to buy!
  How much for Fame! How much for Fame!
Hear how it thunders! would you stand
  On high Olympus, far renowned,
Now purchase, and a world command!--
  And be with a world's curses crowned!

Sweet star of Hope! with ray to shine
  In every sad foreboding breast,
Save this desponding one of mine,
  Who bids for man's last friend and best!
Ah, were not mine a bankrupt life,
  This treasure should my soul sustain;
But Hope and I are now at strife,
  Nor ever may unite again.

And SONG!—For sale my tuneless lute.
  Sweet solace, mine no more to hold;
The chords that charmed my soul are mute,
  I cannot wake the notes of old!
Or e'en were mine a wizard shell,
  Could chain a world in raptures high;
Yet now a sad farewell!—farewell!
  Must on its last faint echoes die.

WORLD-SALE.

Ambition, fashion, show, and pride,
I part from all for ever now;
Grief, in an overwhelming tide,
Has taught my haughty heart to bow.
Poor heart! distracted, ah, so long,
And still its aching throb to bear;
How broken, that was once so strong;
How heavy, once so free from care.

Ah, cheating earth!—could man but know,
Sad soul of mine, what thou and I,—
The bud would never wish to blow,
The nestling never long to fly!
Perfuming the regardless air;
High soaring into empty space;
A blossom ripening to despair,
A flight—without a resting place!

No more for me life's fitful dream;
Bright vision, vanishing away!
My bark requires a deeper stream;
My sinking soul a surer stay.
By death, stern sheriff! all bereft,
I weep, yet humbly kiss the rod;
The best of all I still have left,—
My Faith, my Bible, and my God.

OLD.

OLD.—An Aged Stranger resting by the Road-Side—His Antique Apparel—School-Children at Play—Isabel—Sad Reminiscences—Old School-House—Birthplace—Sycamore Trees—Orchard—Fields—Flocks—Grain—Fishing—Mill—Cottage—Mary Jane—Church—Marriage—Conclusion.

OLD.

Buckled knee and shoe, and broad-rimmed hat,
Coat as ancient as the form 'twas folding,
Silver buttons, queue, and crimped cravat,
Oaken staff his feeble hand upholding,
There he sat!
Buckled knee and shoe, and broad-rimmed hat.

OLD

A RURAL SKETCH.

BY the way-side, on a mossy stone,
  Sat a hoary pilgrim sadly musing;
Oft I marked him sitting there alone,
  All the landscape like a page perusing;
      Poor, unknown,
By the way-side, on a mossy stone.

OLD.

Buckled knee and shoe, and broad-rimmed hat,
  Coat as ancient as the form 'twas folding,
Silver buttons, queue, and crimped cravat,
  Oaken staff, his feeble hand upholding,
    There he sat!
Buckled knee and shoe, and broad-rimmed hat.

Seemed it pitiful he should sit there,
  No one sympathizing, no one heeding,
None to love him for his thin grey hair,
  And the furrows all so mutely pleading
    Age and care;
Seemed it pitiful he should sit there.

It was summer, and we went to school,
  Dapper country lads and little maidens,
Taught the motto of the "Dunce's Stool,"
  Its grave import still my fancy ladens,
    "Here's a fool!"
It was summer, and we went to school.

Still, in sooth, our tasks we seldom tried;
  Sportive pastime only worth our learning,
But we listened when the old man sighed,
  And that lesson to our hearts went burning,
    And we cried!
Still, in sooth, our tasks we seldom tried.

OLD.

When the stranger seemed to mark our play,
  (Some of us were joyous, some sad-hearted,)
I remember, well,—too well,—that day!
  Oftentimes the tears unbidden started,
    Would not stay!
When the stranger seemed to mark our play.

When we cautiously adventured nigh
  We could see his lip with anguish quiver:
Yet no word he uttered, but his eye
  Seemed in mournful converse with the river
    Murmuring by,
When we cautiously adventured nigh.

One sweet spirit broke the silent spell,
  Ah! to me her name was always heaven!
She besought him all his grief to tell,
  (I was then thirteen, and she eleven,)
    Isabel!
One sweet spirit broke the silent spell.

Softly asked she with a voice divine,
  Why so lonely hast thou wandered hither;
Hast no home?—then come with me to mine;
  There's our cottage, let me lead thee thither;
    Why repine,
Softly asked she with a voice divine.

OLD.

Angel, said he sadly, I am old:
  Earthly hope no longer hath a morrow
Yet why I sit here thou shalt be told,
  Then his eye betrayed a pearl of sorrow;
    Down it rolled;
Angel, said he sadly, I am old!

I have tottered here to look once more
  On the pleasant scene where I delighted
In the careless, happy days of yore,
  Ere the garden of my heart was blighted
    To the core!
I have tottered here to look once more!

All the picture now to me how dear!
  E'en this grey old rock where I am seated,
Seems a jewel worth my journey here;
  Ah, that such a scene should be completed
    With a tear!
All the picture now to me how dear!

Old stone School-house !—it is still the same!
  There's the very step so oft I mounted;
There's the window creaking in its frame,
  And the notches that I cut and counted
    For the game:
Old stone School-house!—it is still the same!

OLD.

In the cottage yonder I was born;
  Long my happy home—that humble dwelling;
There the fields of clover, wheat, and corn,
  There the spring with limpid nectar swelling;
    Ah, forlorn!—
In the cottage yonder I was born.

Those two gate-way sycamores you see
  Then were planted, just so far asunder
That long well-pole from the path to free,
And the wagon to pass safely under;
    Ninety-three!
Those two gate-way sycamores you see.

There's the orchard where we used to climb
  When my mates and I were boys together,
Thinking nothing of the flight of time,
  Fearing nought but work and rainy weather;
    Past its prime!
There's the orchard where we used to climb!

There the rude three-cornered chestnut rails,
  Round the pasture where the flocks were grazing,
Where so sly I used to watch for quails
  In the crops of buckwheat we were raising,
    Traps and trails,
There the rude three-cornered chestnut rails.

OLD.

How in summer have I traced that stream,
  There through mead and woodland sweetly gliding,
Luring simple trout with many a scheme
  From the nooks where I have found them hiding;
          All a dream!
How in summer have I traced that stream.

There's the mill that ground our yellow grain;
  Pond, and river still serenely flowing;
Cot, there nestling in the shaded lane,
  Where the lily of my heart was blowing,—
          MARY JANE!
There's the mill that ground our yellow grain!

There's the gate on which I used to swing,
  Brook, and bridge, and barn, and old red stable:
But, alas! the morn shall no more bring
  That dear group around my father's table;
          Taken wing!
There's the gate on which I used to swing!

I am fleeing!—all I loved are fled;
  Yon green meadow was our place for playing;
That old tree can tell of sweet things said,
  When around it Jane and I were straying;
          She is dead!
I am fleeing!—all I loved are fled!

OLD.

Yon white spire—a pencil on the sky,
Tracing silently life's changeful story,
So familiar to my dim old eye,
Points me to seven that are now in glory
There on high!
Yon white spire, a pencil on the sky.

Oft the aisle of that old church we trod,
Guided thither by an angel mother,
Now she sleeps beneath its sacred sod,
Sire and sisters, and my little brother;
Gone to God!
Oft the aisle of that old church we trod!

There I heard of Wisdom's pleasant ways;
Bless the holy lesson!—but, ah, never
Shall I hear again those songs of praise,
Those sweet voices silent now forever!
Peaceful days!
There I heard of Wisdom's pleasant ways.

There my Mary blest me with her hand,
When our souls drank in the nuptial blessing,
Ere she hastened to the spirit land:
Yonder turf her gentle bosom pressing:
Broken band!
There my Mary blest me with her hand.

OLD

I have come to see that grave once more.
  And the sacred place where we delighted.
Where we worshipped in the days of yore,
  Ere the garden of my heart was blighted
    To the core!
I have come to see that grave once more.

Haply, ere the verdure there shall fade,
  I, all withering with years, shall perish;
With my Mary may I there be laid,
  Join forever—all the wish I cherish—
    Her dear Shade!—
Haply, ere the verdure there shall fade.

Angel, said he sadly, I am old!
  Earthly hope no longer hath a morrow;
Now why I sit here thou hast been told;
  In his eye another pearl of sorrow,—
    Down it rolled!
Angel, said he sadly, I am old!

By the way-side, on a mossy stone,
  Sat the hoary pilgrim, sadly musing.
Still I marked him sitting there alone,
  All the landscape like a page perusing;
    Poor, unknown,
By the way-side, on a mossy stone.

NEW.

NEW.—Love of Novelty—Will-o'-Wisp—Fleeting Pleasures—Phantom—Youthful Hope—The Rose—Discontent—May Skies—June Flowers—Summer—October—Viper—Fashion—The Fickle Fair—The Swain—The Task—Desire for Manhood—Ambition—Success—Beauty—Home—Still Unsatisfied—Phantasies—Still Something New.

NEW,

A PORTRAITURE OF DISCONTENT.

Still sighs the world for something new
For something new;
Imploring me, imploring you,
Some Will-o'-wisp to help pursue;
Ah, hapless world, what will it do!
Imploring me, imploring you,
For something new!

Each pleasure, tasted, fades away,
It fades away;
Nor you nor I can bid it stay;
A dew-drop trembling on a spray;
A rainbow at the close of day;
Nor you nor I can bid it stay;
It fades away!

NEW.

Fill up life's chalice to the brim ;
        Up to the brim ;
'Tis only a capricious whim ;
    A dreamy phantom, flitting dim,
Inconstant still for Her, or Him ;
    'Tis only a capricious whim,
        Up to the brim !

SHE.

SHE, young and fair, expects delight ;
        Expects delight ;
Forsooth, because the morn is bright,
    She deems it never will be night,
That youth hath not a wing for flight,
    Forsooth, because the morn is bright,
        Expects delight !

The rose, once gathered, cannot please ,
        It cannot please ;
Ah, simple maid, a rose to seize,
    That only blooms to tempt and teaze :
With thorns to rob the heart of ease ;
    Ah, simple maid, a rose to seize ;
        It cannot please !

NEW.

'Tis winter, but she pines for spring;
She pines for spring;
No bliss its frost and follies bring;
A bird of passage on the wing;
Unhappy, discontented thing
No bliss its frost and follies bring;
She pines for spring!

Delicious May, and azure skies,
And azure skies;
With flowers of paradisial dyes;
Now, maiden, happy be and wise:
Ah, JUNE can only charm her eyes
With flowers of paradisial dyes,
And azure skies!

The glowing, tranquil summertime,
The Summer-time;
Too listless in a maiden's prime,
Dull, melancholy pantomime;
Oh, for a gay autumnal clime:
Too listless in a maiden's prime.
The Summer-time!

NEW.

October! with earth's richest store;
        Earth's richest store!
Alas, insipid as before;
  Days, months, and seasons, o'er and o'er
Remotest lands their treasures pour;
  Alas, insipid as before,
        Earth's richest store!

Love nestles in that gentle breast;
        That gentle breast;
Ah, love will never let it rest!
  The cruel, sly, ungrateful guest;
A viper in a linnet's nest;
  Ah, love will never let it rest;
        That gentle breast!

Could she embark on Fashion's tide;
        On fashion's tide;
How gaily might a maiden glide;—
  Contentment, innocence, and pride,
All stranded upon either side!—
  How gaily might a maiden glide,
        On fashion's tide!

NEW.

Ah, maiden, time will make thee smart;
    Will make thee smart;
Some new, and keen, and poisoned dart,
  Will pierce at last that restless heart;
Youth, friends, and beauty will depart;
  Some new, and keen, and poisoned dart,
    Will make thee smart!

So pants for change the fickle fair;
    The fickle fair;
A feather floating in the air,
  Still wafted here, and wafted there,
No charm, no hazard worth her care;
  A feather floating in the air,
    The fickle Fair!

HE.

How sad his lot, the hapless swain;
    The hapless Swain;
With care, and toil, in heat and rain,
  To speed the plough or harvest-wain,
Still reaping only fields of grain,
  With care, and toil, in heat and rain;
    The hapless Swain!

Must bear, alas, parental rule ;
        Parental rule ;
The tiresome task ; the irksome school ;
    His life is but a passive pool ;
O, were he but a man !—(the fool !)
    The tiresome task, the irksome school,
        Parental rule !

Youth, weary youth, 'twill soon be past ;
        'Twill soon be past ;
His MANHOOD'S happiness shall last ;
    Renown, and riches, far and fast,
Their potent charms shall round him cast,
    His Manhood's happiness shall last :—
        'Twill soon be past !

Now toiling up ambition's steep ;
        Ambition's steep ;
The rugged path is hard to keep ;
    The spring how far ! the well how deep !
Ah me ! in folly's bower asleep !
    The rugged path is hard to keep ;
        Ambition's steep !

NEW.

The dream fulfilled! rank, fortune, fame;
Rank, fortune, fame;
Vain fuel for celestial flame!
He wins and wears a glittering name,
Yet sighs his longing soul the same;
Vain fuel for celestial flame,
Rank, fortune, fame!

Sweet Beauty aims with Cupid's Bow;
With Cupid's bow;
Can she transfix him now?—ah, no!
Amid the fairest flowers that blow,
The torment but alights—to go;
Can she transfix him now?—ah, no,
With Cupid's bow!

Indulgent heaven grant but this,
O grant but this,
The boon shall be enough of bliss,
A HOME, with true affection's kiss,
To mend whate'er may hap amiss,
The boon shall be enough of bliss;
O grant but this!

NEW.

The Eden won :—insatiate still,
Insatiate still ;—
A wider, fairer range, he will ;
Some mountain higher than his hill ;
Some prospect fancy's map to fill ;
A wider, fairer range he will ;
Insatiate still !

From maid to matron, son to sire ;
From son to sire,
Each bosom burns with quenchless fire,
Where life's vain phantasies expire
In some new phœnix of desire ;
Each bosom burns with quenchless fire,
From son to sire !

Still sighs the world for something new,
For something new ;
Imploring me, imploring you,
Some Will-o'-wisp to help pursue ;
Ah, hapless world, what will it do ;
Imploring me, imploring you,
For SOMETHING NEW !

RAIN.

RAIN.—The Valley—Scenery—Summer—Harvest—Reapers Asleep—Ox Standing in the Brook—Noontide Repose—Thunder Beyond the Mountains—Rising of the Wind—Drops of Rain—Haste to Reach Home—Homestead—Reminiscences—Rain in Torrents—Scampering of Cattle—Leisure for Stories—Piety—Reviving Flowers—The Willow—The Inn—Wagon from School—Approach of Evening—Fanny—Kate—Stranger—Barn-Yard—Night—The End.

RAIN.

Yonder, at the Inn, together
  Fast a wayside group collecting,
Much discourse of rainy weather,
  Idle almanacs rejecting,
    Boy and man
Each predicting all he can.

RAIN.

A SUMMER REMINISCENCE.

In the valley, I remember,
  Where my life's bright morn was glowing,
Summer-morning!—no December
  Wintry gales of sorrow blowing;
    Wilton dale!
All was bliss in that sweet vale!

There were gently sloping meadows,
  Where sweet streams went softly gliding,
Sunny glades and forest shadows,
  All in beauty there abiding:
    Simple swain,
Most of all I loved—the Rain!

RAIN.

Summer!—lies the fragrant clover
   Where the harvestmen were reaping,
But the morning task is over,
   And the laborers are sleeping:
         It is noon,
In the sultry time of June.

'Mid the brook that murmurs yonder,
   Deep the weary ox is wading
To the cool retreat, far under
   Where the arching boughs o'ershading,
         Shun the fly,
Tiresome yoke, and burning sky.

Happy valley!—so serenely
   Morning's toilsome season closing;
E'en the scythe, that mowed so keenly,
   Rake, and haystack seem reposing;
         Vale and hill,
Rural noontide—warm and still.

Long the thirsty fields have waited,
   Of refreshing nectar dreaming;
But the tokens have abated,
   Every hope fallacious seeming;
         Drooping low,
All the harvests mourn the wo.

RAIN.

Voice beyond the mountains!—harken!
Nature's awful bass is pealing;
Clouds the fair horizon darken,
Over all the valley stealing—
Up!—prepare!—
There's a deluge in the air!

Now the distant woods awaken,
Where the gusty wind is calling;
Now the nearer trees are shaken,
And the great round drops are falling;
Take the lane!—
There will be a drenching rain!

Homestead!—ours was very lowly,
Rafters on the lattice pressing;
Yet, though humble, it seemed holy—
For, when God sent down his blessing
From the cloud,
The old roof would sing aloud!

With the past as memory mingles,
Often yet mine ear is listening
For that anthem of the shingles!—
Hopeful—till mine eye is glistening
With this truth—
Gone the music of my youth!

RAIN.

Now descends the brimming fountain!
  Window, door and eaves are dripping;
O'er the pasture, up the mountain,
  Scampering cattle soon outstripping—
    Onward yet—
All the landscape drowning wet!

Leisure now for jest and story,
  Village news, or song, or reading,
Ballad tales of love and glory;
  All the clattering storm unheeding,
    Let it pour,—
Cannot reach the old oak floor!

Peace within that household ever;
  Love's sweet rule each breast controlling;
Truth's high precepts broken never:
  What though clouds around are rolling—
    Let them roll—
Theirs the sunshine of the soul!

Matchless painter!—leaf and flower
  All their faded hues reviving;
How the garden drinks the shower,
  Life and loveliness deriving;
    Grove and glade
All in sprightly pearls arrayed.

RAIN.

E'en less mournful yon lone willow,
  By the churchyard ever weeping;
And the daisies o'er each pillow
  Where the blessed dead are sleeping,
      Seem to say—
We revive—and so will they!

Yonder, at the Inn, together
  Fast a wayside group collecting;
Much discourse of rainy weather,
  Idle almanacs rejecting,
      Boy and man
Each predicting all he can.

Hark the ring of happy voices;
  Wagon from the school appearing;
How each drowning imp rejoices,
  As the puzzled team go veering
      Gee, and haw,
With the noisy load they draw.

Slowly eventide advances,
  Fanny at the window reading,
Slyly from the casement glances;—
  Who the youth the storm unheeding,
      At the gate?—
Blushes Fanny—whispers Kate.

RAIN.

Is he stranger worn with travel,
  Refuge from the torrent seeking?
Timid looks the doubt unravel,
  Looks all eloquently speaking!
      Happy guest,
With a welcome so confest!

Earnest he apologizes,
  From the mill in haste returning,
(Oh, forgive young love's disguises,
  Though it rains, his heart is burning;)
      He will stay
Just a moment on his way.

Now the motley barnyard nation,
  Cackling, lowing, neighing, squealing,
Crowd at their accustomed station,
  For the evening fare appealing;
      Hastens Ned,
And the poor wet things are fed.

Slowly spread the shades of even;
  Night, on raven wing descended,
Shuts the mighty doors of heaven;
  And, the landscape's glory ended,
      Ends the Lay,
Happy—rural—Rainy day.

SHOWER.

In a valley that I know,—
Happy scene!
There are meadows sloping low,
There the fairest flowers blow,
And the brightest waters flow,
All serene;
But the sweetest thing to see,
If you ask the dripping tree,
Or the harvest-hoping swain,
Is the Rain!

Ah, the dwellers of the town,
How they sigh,
How ungratefully they frown
When the cloud-king shakes his crown.
And the pearls come pouring down
From the sky!
They descry no charm at all
Where the sparkling jewels fall,
And each moment of the snower,
Seems an hour.

SHOWER.

Yet there's something very sweet
        In the sight,
When the crystal currents meet,
In the dry and dusty street,
And they wrestle with the heat,
        In their might!
While they seem to hold a talk
With the stones along the walk,
And remind them of the rule,
        To "keep cool!"

But in that quiet dell,
        Ever fair,
Still the Lord doth all things well,
When His clouds with blessings swell,
And they break a brimming shell
        On the air;
There the Shower hath its charms
Sweet and welcome to the farms,
As they listen to its voice
        Ana rejoice!

OUTALISSA.

Outalissa.—Seneca Lake—Tempest Arising—Night—Fierce Wild Beasts—Weary Traveller—Indian Hospitality—Morning—Grand Scenery—Ascent of Outalee—Aged Chief's Prediction—Appeal to the White Man—The Sacred Pledge—The Temptation—Ingratitude—The Catastrophe.

OUTALISSA,

A TRADITION OF SENENCA LAKE

Note.—[SENECA LAKE, on which the town of Geneva is situated, is perhaps the most picturesque sheet of water in our State. It is about forty-one miles long, and two miles wide; embellished with the most romantic scenery, furnishing at every point fine subjects for the pen or for the pencil. The water rises and falls a few inches at regular intervals; a phenomenon not accounted for in this, nor observed in our other lakes. Dead bodies never float upon its surface, but its extreme transparency often reveals what, like a subtle murderer, it would never otherwise confess. A large tree has been floating up and down, from end to end of this beautiful lake, during many years, and it is now regarded with much interest by the ancient dwellers of the neighborhood, from whom tho writer gathered the wild tradition concerning it, which, in the following poem. he has endeavored to preserve.]

OUTALISSA.

The tempest gathering fierce and fast
  Darkly the welkin overcast;
The sun was o'er the western hill;
  And autumn winds blew chill;
The ominous melancholy owl
  Screamed to the prowling panther's howl
The wolf lay lurking in his lair,
  Scenting the treacherous air.

By Seneca, that wildly tossed,
  A weary stranger, lone and lost,
Pursued his dismal, dangerous way,
  Seeking a place to lay
His fainting neart and aching head,
  And sleep the slumber of the dead;

Praying only that he might die
  Screened from each monster's eye.

As sadly onward still he pressed,
  Deep anguish brooding in his breast,
The last hope quenching in despair,—
  " Yaicomah !—who comes there ?"
A forest-voice demanded mild !—
  " Peace to the wanderer of the wild !
Rest, stranger,—hide thee from the blast
  Till this drear night be past.
In Outalissa's friendly cell,
  The white man shall securely dwell,
Shall sit upon the welcome-seat,
  And share his children's meat."
To where a taper dimly burned,
  The worn wayfarer fainting turned,
And soon within the red man's door
  Slept, all his sorrows o'er.

Went past the night,—went past the storm ;
The morning sun came bright and warm
Adown on hill, and vale, and wood,
Cheering the mighty solitude.

OUTALISSA.

Where grew the sacred Council-Tree,
Upon the verge of Outalee,
The chieftain and the guest ascend,
And free in social converse blend;
Beguiling still the toilsome way
With kindest words that each could say,
Till, from the summit's lofty crown,
They on the scene below looked down,
Far-gazing, as o'er half the globe,
On nature in her fairest robe;
Old forests, dells, and silver streams,
It seemed but Fancy's land of dreams,
A glorious inspiring sight—
A world all bathed in living light!

But deeply now the patriarch sighed,
And, o'er the lovely vision, cried
" Alas, that these old eyes should see,
Home of my sires, thy destiny!
Mark, stranger! When these limbs are still,
When Outalissa's heart is chill,
When his fleet arrow flies no more
By Seneca's wild mountain shore,
Then this fair landscape shall be thine;

The white man's sword these fields of mine
Will stain with the poor Indian's blood ;
Each rivulet will be a flood
Swoll'n with our wives' and orphans' tears !
Ah, that these eyes should see those years !
That I, prophetic, should behold
The wolf in my defenceless fold,
And unavenged, foredoomed to die,
My trusty warriors lifeless lie !

Oh stranger, that dark hour I see,
Yet turns my heart in hope to thee ;
Say, when the red man's hut shall blaze,
And thy white brothers fierce shall raise
The long, annihilating knife,
Wilt thou protect my widowed wife ;
My comely, dark-eyed daughter save
From brutal hands, if not the grave.
But ah, too much from thee I ask ;
'Twere e'en for me a mighty task,
Though I were then as firm to be,
And stalwart, as this Council-Tree :
I would not, stranger, ask thee swear
To see fulfilled a hopeless prayer,

But this one boon I joy to know
Thou canst and freely wilt bestow ;
Take this green branch, and o'er it bend,
And swear to be the Indian's friend !

Then thrice the stranger bowed him o'er
The mystic misletoe and swore,
" By Manitou that hears me vow,
By yon bright orb that sees me bow,
By the deep lake beneath our feet,
By heaven above, that marks deceit,
And by this sacred Tree, whose shade
A solemn council-hall is made,
Eternal love to thee and thine
Shall warm this grateful heart of mine !"

" Enough !" the aged Sachem said,
And pensive drooped his silvered head ;
Sad thoughts oppressed his heart,—he wept,
Then leaned against the tree, and slept.

Now noon was glowing on the hills,
The herds were laving in the rills,
The lake, rejoicing in its sheen,

Reflected all the golden scene,
The sky was cloudless, and the breeze
Came odorous o'er sweet-scented trees,
'Twas, near and far, a fair domain
A monarch might be proud to gain.

Then rushed upon the stranger's soul,
Temptation dark,—'tis but to roll
The sleeping chief beyond the brink
And all is mine !—'tis but a link
That, breaking, I shall sooner buy
What must be mine by prophecy.

The spell had power !—Oh gratitude,
Where then thy thunderbolts !—he viewed
The slumber deepening on the eye,
Watched the last, sad, foreboding sigh,
Till all in quiet sleep were stilled,
Then crept, a murderer, staunch and skilled,
And the dread perjury fulfilled !

The deed was seen in heaven, and swift
The Spirit-Senecas uplift
Their vengeful prayer :—Oh ! Manitou !

That see'st o'er all the world below,
And mark'st the ingrate, and deceit,
Let flee the whirlwind from thy feet!
But e'er that prayer had reached the throne,
The dire, avenging blast was down!
Clutched the foul wretch, and reft the tree
That shadowed o'er the perjury,
And instant, as the lightning's flash,
Down, down the craggy steep they crash!
Till from the jutting rock they take
The last wild bound and reach the lake!
Th' astonished water hastes to hide
The twain intruders in its tide;
Mid-depth they part,—the villain white
Sinks to the caves,—the tree, to sight
Its way with swift ascension wins,
And its long wandering begins.

The sires of Seneca are dead,
A thousand moons have come and fled,
Their hunting seasons all are past,
Yet still that Council-Tree shall last,
And as it journeys still complain—
"I SAW GREAT OUTALISSA SLAIN!"

BLACKSMITH'S NIGHT.

Blacksmith's Night.—Welcome Hour of Rest—Sunset—Invocation—Toil—Luxury—Unrequited Labor—Despondency—Approach of a Sombre Figure—Addresses the Blacksmith—Wraps him in a Mantle of utter Darkness—Encouragement—Dignity of Man—Work, Meritorious—Ultimate Reward—The Vision Vanishes—Morning Returns—A Christian Hero.

BLACKSMITH'S NIGHT.

Yet as from my low smithy now I gaze,
  Far to the eaves of his great shop sublime
Still seems his mighty furnace all a-blaze,
    Still seems to chime
His ponderous anvil with the sledge of Time!

THE

BLACKSMITH'S NIGHT.

O WELCOME hour when peaceful eve once more
  Spreads her dun curtain for a world's repose;
Bids him be free who was a slave before,
          And for his woes
Her mystic balm, oblivious sleep, bestows.

All hushed the landscape, and the sinking sun
  Like a tired giant closes for the night
The wondrous labor he again hath done,
          In his swift flight,
Girding the earth anew with hoops of light!

Yet as from my low smithy now I gaze,
  Far to the eaves of his great shop sublime,
Still seems his mighty furnace all a-blaze,
          Still seems to chime
His ponderous anvil with the sledge of Time!

His sky-wide window in the west how red
  As with some molten metal's fiery glow!
And how the cinders glitter overhead,
          In starry show,
As far their twinkling radiance they throw!

Laborious Phoebus! with long ages gray,
  What sudden chance requires his toilful skill?
Hath earth's old groaning axis given way?
          Or doth he still
Repair some wheel, o'erstrained up Morn's steep hill!

Or doth he now his furious steeds reshoe,
  To climb again the azure arch on high;
Or at his fire his tarnished rays renew,
          Ere he can fly
To scatter light along to-morrow's sky!

Or lonely on some dim Hesperian brink,
Doth he reluctant eye the darkening Deep,
In sad incertitude to plunge or shrink;
Constrained to leap,
Yet shuddering o'er the fearful flood to sweep!

Roll down, O Sun! thy lingering beams no more
Bring tranquil twilight nor sweet peace to me,
I love the season when thy reign is o'er;
O Phoebus flee!
And let the Dark in solemn grandeur—be!

Now smoky shadows the horizon skim,
And yonder hills fast fading in the west,
Sing to the dusky air a parting hymn;
And sweet to rest,
Night soothes all nature on her Ethiop breast!

Eternal Darkness! would its shades were mine!
Might I no more life's dreary day behold!
No more to cringe or crave at wealth's proud shrine
For bread or gold,
Crushing my heart in labor's abject mould!

BLACKSMITH'S NIGHT.

How, ere the waking winds shall fan the east,
And on the forge of Morning rouse its flame,
Must my most welcome slumber long have ceased,
And here these same
O'ertasking bellows every sinew claim!

How idle he, the lord of yonder dome,
Yet see the gorgeous pomp his halls display;
No care, no want e'er enters that proud home,
While, wo the day,
My sternest toil drives not the fiends away!

There rolls a chariot to that house of mirth;
These hands of mine prepared the sumptuous car
Yet less it serves to gladden my poor hearth,
Than yon lone star,
Now beaming through my casement from afar!

Why had I not my birth in that bright sphere,
To be an equal with the blest above;
Or why do thought and feeling haunt me here;
Why do I love?—
A wounded Eagle wedded with a Dove!

BLACKSMITH'S NIGHT.

Ah, broken pinion! ah, my famished nest!
  And thou, my gentle mate, well-tried and true,
How would I wring the life-blood from my breast
          To win for you
The needful wealth I cannot even woo!

O prisoned lion! dull, degraded slave!
  Come blackest midnight hide my grief and shame!
Or take me now thou deep oblivious grave,
          And let my name
Perish forever, with this fettered frame!

But lo! a form there rises to my view,
  And o'er the plain comes silently and fast;
Deep folding drapery of inky hue
          Around it cast,
From earth to heaven looming dread and vast!

It is the sable Power I dared to call;
  The Majesty of Night august comes near!
The dreadful Presence doth my soul appal,
          Yet now I hear
A kindly voice soft saying—Do not fear!

BLACKSMITH'S NIGHT.

O, son of toil, no more shalt thou repine:
  I come to show how happy, good and great
Thou can'st be even in this lot of thine,
    This low estate,
Smitten beneath the hammer of thy fate!

My ebon mantle now shall close thee round,
  And thou shalt tread within that dark abyss,
Where, haply, some sweet solace may be found,
    Some quiet bliss,
Some better life than thou hast known in this!

Be thine the pomp of utter darkness now;
  No impious eye shall on thy rest intrude;
No tyrant task shall make thy spirit bow;
    By none pursued;
Thyself sole monarch—reign in solitude!

Primeval Night! Infinitude of gloom!
  My prayer fulfilled, yet brings it no release!
O for the deeper shadow of the tomb,
    Its dreamless peace,
Where the last throb of my sad heart may cease!

Yet thrills that voice again the murky air,
  Never a midnight but there came a morn!
Up from the dungeon now of thy despair,
      For thou wast born
To conquer sorrow, and all fear to scorn!

To thee is granted to behold how Truth
  Links the strong worker with the happy skies
In care's deep furrows plants immortal youth,
      And gives the prize
Of endless glory to the bravely wise!

Centre thou art and Soul of a domain
  Vast as thy utmost wish could e'er desire
Struggle! the Spirit never strives in vain;
      Can ne'er expire;
Up for thy sceptre! take thy throne of fire!

For man is regal when his strength is tried;
  When spirit wills all matter must obey;
Sweeps the resistless mandate like a tide
      Away, away,
Till earth and heaven feel the potent sway!

BLACKSMITH'S NIGHT.

Now as this rayless gloom aside I fling,
  Thy realm of action spreading on the view
Calls to the sooty Blacksmith—be a king!
        Thy reign renew;
Grasping thy mace again, arise and DO!

And as the massive hammer thunders down,
  Shaping the stubborn iron to the plan,
Know that each stroke adds lustre to thy crown,
        And yon wide span
Of gazing planets shout—behold a MAN!

A glorious Man! and thy renown shall be
  Borne by the winds and waters through all time,
While there's a keel to carve it on the sea
        From clime to clime,
Or God ordains that Idleness is Crime!

Then passed the Vision; and the morn once more
  Called up the dreaming smith from his repose;
All calm his heart, so turbulent before;
        And he arose,
A Christian hero—ready for his foes!

ANGEL.

THE ANGEL.—A Low Sad Voice—Bright Cloud—Its Near Approach —A Celestial Being—Enchanting Music—The Angel Pauses on a Sunbeam—The Sad Voice Again—Human Misery—Captivity—Hunger—Separation—False Love—War—Widowhood—Unkindness to Strangers—Unrequited Toil—Neglected Genius—Betrayal —Death of Children—Deserted Age—The Heavenly Solace.

THE

ANGEL.

Was heard, 'tis said, one tranquil eve,
  A low, sad voice along the sky!
(Alas, can heavenly natures grieve,
  Can holy angels weep on high,
And sinless seraphs learn to sigh?)

There spread a cloud of golden hue
  And curtained day's declining light;
Down floating from the distant blue
  It came with strange mysterious flight,
A summer cloud serene and bright.

A form upon celestial wings!
  Wherever pressed her glittering feet
Came gushing forth from hidden strings
  Soft music earth can ne'er repeat,
Melodious concords grandly sweet!

THE ANGEL.

She paused, and on a sunbeam stood,
  Above a gently sloping hill;
Mute wonder fell on field, and wood,
  The gurgling brook and gleesome rill;
And e'en the warbling birds were still.

But that sad voice along the sky
  Yet burdened all the passing gale:
Ah! do the loved in heaven die,
  Doth hope in those fair regions fail?
Sweet Angel, why that plaintive wail!

She gazed o'er all the haunts of men,
  And saw how sorrow's fountains flow:
Gay city, or secluded glen,
  No refuge from the certain blow,
The cruel wound, the hopeless wo.

Amid the proud voluptuous throng
  Mourned many a breaking heart alone,
Crushed in the grasp of want and wrong,
  The sordid world all heedless grown;
Ah, heartless earth! Ah, world of stone!

THE ANGEL.

The captive pining in his chain,
  The famished vainly asking bread ;
Sad partings ne'er to meet again,
  Love's rose that once sweet odors shed,
In youth's bright path, perfumeless, dead.

O'er field and hill, by wave and coast,
  A shout of furious onset rose,
The shock of many a mighty host,
  The struggle of defiant foes
Met in terrific battle-throes!

How red the rivulets shall be :
  How weltering all the rural plain ;
To mingle there that sanguine sea,
  How many a heart its ruddy rain
In that wild strife will pour—in vain!

She saw, where, by the pallet side,
  While orphan babes unconscious slept,
A scanty pittance to provide
  The widow toilsome vigil kept,
And in her watching ceaseless wept.

THE ANGEL.

The weary stranger sought for rest,
  (Ah, who the goal hath ever won ?)
No door was opened for a guest,
  None wished the pilgrim's journey done,
Nor made life's race less sad to run !

From rugged Labor's earnest hand
  Uprose the palace, teemed the soil ;
And navies launched at his command,
  For lordly Indolence a spoil ;
Ah, hapless, unrequited Toil !

How many a generous bosom burned,
  With all sublime aspirings fraught,
Yet ever found its fervor spurned :
  Rich with the jewelry of thought,
Yet all its worth accounted Nought.

Where mournful sighed a maniac maid
  No lover's voice in music spoke,
Confiding innocence--betrayed !
  Poor heart, what anguish in the stroke
When it could bear no more—and broke !

THE ANGEL.

Where lay a babe in death's cold sleep
  A mother knelt in mad despair;
Alas! the slumber was too deep,
  The spirit heeded not her prayer;
The cherub was no longer there!

With feeble hand deserted Age
  Was tracing in his sightless gloom
This one sad line for that last page,
  That page of stone above his tomb;
Forsaken! O ye Dead, make room!

Thus gazing o'er the haunts of men,
  She saw how sorrow's fountains flow;
Gay city, or secluded glen,
  Still all resistless falls the blow,
The cruel wound, the hopeless wo.

For this, upon that tranquil eve,
  Came that sad voice along the sky;
For these that heavenly one could grieve;
  That Angel from the realms on high,
With hastening wing came down to sigh.

She wept, and on the sunbeam shed
 Celestial tears, divinely blest;
Swift o'er the sky bright rainbows spread;
 Earth saw, and every mournful breast
With holy solace sank to rest.

But that sad voice along the sky
 Yet lingers on the passing gale,
For sorrow's fount is never dry,
 And still, where'er its streams prevail
Sweet PITY pours her plaintive wail.

WHERE.

A GENTLE youth would follow Hope,
 To roam through pleasure's fairy land,
The portals of delight to ope,
 To feast the eye and fill the hand,
To drink of fountains fresh and clear,
 And rest in bowers safe and fair,
But still as oft as hope said—here!
 And bade him seize the bliss so rare,
The disappointed youth said—Where!

WHERE.

He wandered from his native vale,
  Allured by voices from afar,
Soft breezes fanned his ready sail,
  And o'er the wave arose a star;
He trusted then the tranquil sea,
  Some Paradise to seek and share,
But in the fairest Eden, he
  O'erworn with weariness and care,
Still sad and listless murmured—Where!

Then, instant, as he looked beyond,
  Some new temptation would arise,
Some seeming angel fair and fond,
  Some casket that contained the prize,
'Twere but a moment's space to reach,
  The briefest journey here to there,
His arm could soon encompass each,
  Yet as he grasped the empty air,
Some distant cave would echo—Where!

Came Beauty dazzling then his eye,
  And cast her spell around his heart,
E'en midnight seemed a sunlit sky,
  Such glitter did her glance impart,

WHERE.

He sprang enchanted to adore,
  To flutter in her silken snare ;
Alas ! the vision soon was o'er ;
  A blight—and all the bower was bare ;
And Beauty's rose was blooming—Where ?

Then heard he on the air a blast,
  A wildly sweet inspiring strain ;
Aloft a mournful look he cast,
  And there was Hope's bright form again !
Before him rose a rugged steep,
  Its summit bore a temple fair ;
Up ! said Ambition, onward sweep,
  For fame's immortal joys prepare ;
But still his weary heart said—Where !

So tasted he life's choicest wine,
  Wealth, honor, all they can secure ;
Yet did his longing soul repine,
  They were not lasting, true, and pure :
Still seemed the guerdon far above
  The proudest height his foot could dare :
Then came the word of heavenly love,
  By yonder Cross go breathe a prayer,
He knelt, and lo, his REST was There !

SUE.

Sue.—Youthful Days—Clouds of Manhood—The Valley Belle—Hyacinth, my Sue—Kindness—Coyness—Beauty—Summer-Rose—The Brook—Suicidal Look—Nightingale—No Contentment—The Bower—The Lily There—Eventide—Cottage Door—The Suit—The Marriage—Heart's-Ease—Twining Ivy—Increasing Years True Affection—Tranquillity—Hope of Heaven.

SUE.

One serenest eventide,
When the toils of day were o'er,
She was sitting at the side
Of her little cottage door.

SUE,

A TALE OF LASTING LOVE.

In the days when I was young,
  Just a ripple on life's sea,
Ere the clouds of manhood flung
  Their dark shadows over me;
When my spirit was as light
  As my own Green-mountain air,
And my hopes were all as bright
  As the sunbeams shining there,
Oh, how deeply then I fell—
  Fell in love! and so would you,
Had you seen our valley belle,
  That sweet hyacinth, my Sue!

SUE.

She was kind, but she was coy,
  And whenever I came near,
Though a harmless, blushing boy,
  She would shrink as if with fear,
And the lash of her blue eye
  Would its falling form display,
Like the fringe along the sky,
  When the evening shuts the day:
Ah, how she bewitched my heart!
  And, (between myself and you,)
She would sometimes make it smart,
  That sweet summer rose, my Sue

Oh, how often have I sat
  All alone beside the brook,
And have cast away my hat,
  With a suicidal look!
And I might have plunged me in,
  Had not something whispered—nay
And preserved me from that sin,
  To be happy here to-day.
Ah, this drowning is a thing
  It were impious to do,
As I've often heard her sing;
  That sweet nightingale, my Sue.

SUE

And how often have I strayed
  With the lads along the lea,
With many a pretty maid,
  Yet, ah, none of them for me;
For if she, whom I loved best,
  In the groups could not be seen,
No contentment in my breast,
  No delight upon the green;
But there was a garden nigh,
  With its bower just in view,
And still sought my heart and eye,
  That sweet lily there, my Sue.

One serenest eventide,
  When the toils of day were o'er,
She was sitting at the side
  Of her little cottage door:
Then I pressed my suit again
  Like a pilgrim at a shrine,
Oh, it was not all in vain,
  She consented to be mine:
In a moment, with a whirl,
  For the priest away I flew,
And that gentle, joyous girl,
  Was my sweet heart's-ease, my Sue!

And I love her all the more,
  Now tnat she has come to be
Like the ivy, twining o'er
  This old gray-grown turret, me!
Neither have I one regret,
  As I mark the flying years,
For she clings the closer yet
  As the faster fall the tears;
And she looks with me above,
  With a clear and tranquil view,
For an endless life of love,
  My sweet hyacinth, my Sue.

RETURN.

All welcome to my heart,
  My own sweet bird,
No more shalt thou depart,
  My first preferred!
I bade through all thy flight,
  Love's beacon burn,
And called, the weary night,
  Return! Return!

RETURN

'Twas gloomy all the day,
  While thou wast flown,
And voiceless things would say
  Alone! Alone!
When sad I op'd the door
  And gazed around,
Where oftentimes before,
  I thee had found.

How desolate our cot,
  The silent hearth
Its busy blaze forgot,
  And all its mirth.
And often did I trace
  Our flowery walk,
But ah, the chiefest grace
  Had left its stalk.

The simple little flower,
  I loved so well,
In some far distant bower
  Was gone to dwell;
I could not trace thy track,
  But prayed a prayer
Some breeze might waft thee back
  My flower, my fair!

Now thou again art home,
  My own blue bell,
My own sweet bird is come
  I loved so well.
And long the day shall be
  Ere thou wilt part,
To roam again so free,
  From my fond heart.

SHADOW

Fleeting vision! well-a-day,
  Life's a shadow all the way!
If you doubt me, listen now,
  Let me tell you why and how
Shadow, infant; shadow, man;
  Show me substance if you can!
Turn or change it as you may,
  Life's a shadow all the way!

SHADOW.

Infancy assumes a smile,
  Only shadow all the while ;
While we ask if it be truth,
  Childhood verges into youth !
Youth, the time of books and school,
  Dreadful shadow, dreading fool !
Irksome lessons, hard to say,
  Horrid shadows in the way.

Swift we come to man's estate ;
  Would its shadow then but wait !
But it hasteth on to see
  The meridian degree,
O'er the dial of our day
  Pass like morning mist away ;
All the shadow, all the sun
  Gone before they seemed begun !

Cupid slyly aims his dart,
  Pierces through and through the heart ;
How delicious, yet how drear !
  What strange frenzy lurking here ;
Cannot come, nor stay, nor go,
  Some dear shadow haunting so !
Stern as winter, mild as May,
  Neither scared nor coaxed away.

SHADOW.

Shadow oft the wedded life;
  Every boy must have a wife:
Every maiden will be wed,
  Eager heart and simple head,
Sure of happiness complete;
  What a shadow! what deceit!
When the nuptial link is tied,
  Shadow husband! shadow bride!

Folly urges, fashion drives,
  Mortals all their mortal lives;
E'er so gay, or e'er so grand,
  Shadow, and a rope of sand!
Unsubstantial at the best,
  Cannot bear affliction's test;
Turn or change it as we may,
  Life's a shadow all the way!

Yet, be happy, Age and Youth,
  Ye have still the Word of Truth:
No delusive shadow here,
  Firm, consoling, and sincere.
If you doubt me, listen now,
  Let me tell you why and how.
It was spoken from above,
  Word of Truth, and Life, and Love,

O'ER THE HILL.

O'er the Hill.—Young Pilgrim—Flowery Path—Beguiling Voice—The Youth's Reply—Noon—A Wide Plain—The Traveller—Truth—Enticements—Rest in Heaven—Shades of Night—Dark Deep Stream—Sequestered Valley—Aged Christian—The Passage—Home for Ever.

O'ER THE HILL.

ONE morning as he wended
  Through a path bedight with flowers,
Where all delights were blended
  To beguile the fleeting hours,
Sweet Youth, pray turn thee hither,
  Said a voice along the way,
Ere all these roses wither,
  And these fair fruits decay,
But the youth paused not to ponder
  If the voice were good or ill,
For, said he, my home is yonder,
  O'er the hill there, o'er the Hill!

O'ER THE HILL

Again, high noon was glowing
  On a wide and weary plain,
And there, right onward going,
  Was the traveller again:
He seemed another being
  Than the morning's rosy youth,
But I quickly knew him, seeing
  His unaltered brow of truth:
Rest, stranger, rest till even',
  Sang alluring voices still;
But he cried—my rest is heaven!
  O'er the hill there, o'er the Hill!

The shades of night were creeping
  A sequestered valley o'er,
Where a dark, deep stream was sweeping
  By a dim and silent shore;
And there the pilgrim, bending
  With the burthen of the day,
Was seen still onward wending,
  Through a "straight and narrow way:"
He passed the gloomy river
  As it were a gentle rill,
And rested,—home forever!
  O'er the hill there, o'er the Hill!

BIBLE.

Bible !—Blessed Bible !
  Treasure of the heart !
What sweet consolation
  Doth thy page impart ;
In the fiercest trial,
  In the deepest grief,
Strength, and hope, and comfort,
  In each holy leaf.
Bible,—let me clasp thee,
  Anchor of the soul !
When the storm is raging,
  When the waters roll,
When the frowning heavens
  Darken every star,
And no hopeful beacon
  Glimmereth afar,

BIBLE.

Be my refuge, Bible !
  Then be thou my stay,
Guide me on life's billow,
  Light the dreary way,
Tell me of the morrow,
  When a sun shall rise,
That shall glow forever,
  In unclouded skies,
Tell me of that heaven
  In the climes above,
Where the bark rides safely
  In a sea of love.

Bible !—let me clasp thee !
  Chronicle divine,
Of a world's redemption,
  Of a Saviour, mine !
Wisdom for the simple,
  Riches for the poor,
Hope for the desponding,
  For the sick, a cure.
Rest for all the weary,
  Ransom for the slave,
Courage for the fearful,
  Life beyond the grave !

Bible !—Blessed Bible !
  Treasure of the heart,
What sweet consolation
  Doth thy page impart ;—
In the fiercest trial,
  In the deepest grief,
Strength, and hope, and comfort,
  In each holy leaf.

PERIL.

Hither reckless ranger,
  Love's sweet landscape o'er,
Hither !—there is danger
  All thy steps before ;
Wander thou no more !

Hast thou roamed it over
  Many pleasant days ;
Ah, delighted rover,
  Passion still betrays ;
Fatal all her ways !

PERIL.

Sweetly still alluring,
  She may lead thee where
Bliss appears enduring
  And the skies look fair ;
But beware—beware !

In the rosy bower
  Oft is heard a sigh ;
Fragrant though the flower,
  Tempting to the eye,
Thorns are lurking nigh !

'Tis a bright illusion,
  Where thy feet have been ;
Pleasures in profusion
  Lend a passing sheen ;
Changed, how soon the scene !

Look ! and be admonished,
  In thy thoughtless mirth ;
E'er thou find, astonished,
  All the smiles of earth
False and nothing worth.

PERIL.

On yon mountain nourished,
  Rooted on its brow,
Once a tall oak flourished,
  Oak of spreading bough,
Ah, behold it now !

Yesterday it towered
  To the smiling skies !
Prostrate and o'erpowered
  Now how low it lies,
Never more to rise !

Every breeze of heaven
  Met it with a kiss ;
Tender vows were given,
  Ah, heart-breaking bliss,
They were all for this !

Loving words, oft-spoken,
  Zephyrs told that tree ;
Oft its leafy token
  Bore they over sea,
Faithless yet to be !

PERIL.

In the midnight hour,
  Furious and fast,
Came they with the power
  Of the Autumn blast,
Reft the Oak at last !

Shattered now and dying,
  See how they deride ;
All its glories flying
  On the gusty tide ;
Gone the mountain's pride !

So, earth's friendships blended
  Seem a fragile shell,
In a moment rended,
  Guard it ne'er so well,
Mournful truth to tell !

Pilgrim through life's sorrow,
  Hope's deluded Dove,
Wouldst thou find to-morrow
  Pure enduring love,
Speed thy wing above !

THE LAST VENDUE.

THE LAST VENDUE.—A Mental Tour—Chaotic Confusion—Earth one Great Republic—Dismay of the Haughty—Extinction of Dynasties—The Auctioneer—Vendue Began—Reasons for Peremptory Sale—A Crown—Antique Throne—Iron Sceptre—Coil of Chains—Call for a Purchaser—The Final Stroke—Breaking of the Links—Universal Shout of Joy—Earth Becomes an Eden—A Glittering Zone Descends from Heaven—Man Bound to Man by Christian Love.

THE LAST VENDUE,

A SKETCH OF THE PASSING TIMES.

As I was on a journey late, a mental one
I mean,
Around this mighty world of ours, I came
upon a scene
Was so astonishing to see, so comic, grave,
and grand,
I took my note book out with haste and
clambered to a stand
Upon a heap of broken wares, a motley
pile of things,
That seemed they might have once belong-
ed to some old race of kings ;

And heaps on heaps were strewn about, as
far as eye could scan,
Around the fields, along the streams,
where e'er the vision ran ;

LAST VENDUE.

As if some ruthless creditor had levied on
the world,
And kingdoms, thrones, and diadems, were
all to ruin hurled;
Ill-gotten chattles of the powers that were
compelled to "fail,"
And were all brought together there for one
stupendous sale!

Stood side by side the vassal-born, and
they of proudest birth;
No more a slave, no more a lord, in all
Republic earth.
Yet smiled the skies approvingly, and,
every landscape round,
Rich harvests waited but a word, to burst
the teeming ground;
Betokening a coming hour, when, war's red
banner furled,
Abundance, and content would bless a
liberated world.

What may it mean, quoth I to one, this
great grotesque array,
As though the peasant and the prince were
made of kindred clay;
Methinks I see all equal here, the humble
and the proud;
Now what hath moved these haughty heads
to mingle with the crowd?

And whence this huge chaotic mass, here
piled on every hand;
Magnificence and meanness strewn, like
wrecks along a strand,
As, when some direful storm hath swept
the surging ocean o'er,
Fleet, argosy, and tiny bark with ruins line
the shore.

Then lifted he to whom I spake a fixed and
frowning eye,
As to rebuke such questioning, yet deign-
ing no reply;
For, by the tokens at his feet, a crown and
broken mace,
Behold, I was in audience with one of
royal race!
Poor wanderer! I pitying said, and prayed
for him a prayer,
But quick he vanished in the throngs and
rueful tumults there.

Oh, ye ancestral kingly shades, the Cym-
bri, Saxon, Gaul,
Mourn for the towering thrones you reared
to crush your race,—and fall!
Mourn for the Mighty Arm that smote your
majesty, and threw
Your idle splendor to the winds at that
august Vendue!

LAST VENDUE.

A venerable patriarch arose as Auctioneer,
And, though so aged, still his voice could make all nations hear.
'Tis said he is the veteran that first began his trade
When sang the morning stars for joy, and this great globe was made;
And one could never doubt at all, he seemed so hale and well,
That he will live as long as there is aught on earth to sell!

Upon the concourse as he looked, 'twas saddening to view
What wondrous work the withering glance of his keen eye could do.
A countless crowd was gathered there when his great sale began,
Yet every soul was made to feel the look of that old man;
How did he cause all knees to smite, all vigor to decay,
Turning to ashy hue the cheek, the glossy locks to grey!
The great of earth in vain combine against his potent will;
They build their temples and their towers, but he destroys them still.
The very universe 'tis said, by some old sacred seer,

At last shall smoke beneath his touch, dissolve, and disappear!
But his is not the hand supreme; a Mightier than he
Controls his devastating arm by infinite decree;
And when his work shall be fulfilled, his sway will all be o'er,
The heavens and earth shall pass away—and he shall be no more!
Ah me, he is a dread old man! and there he stood and sold
The wrecks of empires with a heart malevolently cold;
Yet oft he gave a sigh or smile that still that word redeems,
To see beneath his hammer fall such sad and strange extremes.

Upon the shattered parapet of some old tower he sprang,
And, planting his red signal there, his thundering call outrang:
Ye multitudes give ear to me, this merchandise survey;
What bargains these for king and clown, what fortunes here to-day!
Oppression is all bankrupt now, and despot sway is done,
For in the chancery above, lo, freedom's plea hath won;

LAST VENDUE.

The famished world has payment claimed
    of its most rightful debt,
And sheriff Revolution hence has palaces
    —"To Let!"
All idle pomp, all princely state, all signs
    of royal rule
Are going, going, now! for man has spurn-
    ed the kingly school;
And the stern lessons he has learned
    through many a weary page,
Matured to mighty deeds, have oped a
    grand Fraternal Age!

A tarnished bauble in his hand then lifted
    he on high,
And cried, Ye crownless potentates, ye
    powerless princes buy!
'Tis somewhat faded, it is true, but still
    it is a crown,
I'll throw the iron sceptre in—'tis going,
    going—down!
And here, the remnant of a Throne—Ye
    sovereigns of the soil,
Buy now the monster that devoured the
    products of your toil!
Once it was bright with burnished gold,
    with quaint devices graced,
But long the lustre has been dimmed, each
    emblem long defaced;
See Justice bearing broken scales; Honor
    and Truth seem dead,

LAST VENDUE.

Power has lost his thunderbolts ; Mercy
and Hope have fled !
How much the antiquated Throne ! who'll
buy the regal seat ;
What bliss to sit there and suppose an
empire at your feet.
Ah ! could they speak, whose once it was
august thereon to reign,
What desperate battle would they bid for
this old Might again.
I cannot dwell, it must be sold, who makes
it now his own ?
Once, twice, the last, 'tis going, gone !—
here, serf, ascend your throne !

Then at his hand a massive coil of pon-
derous chains I saw ;
A sign that men would nevermore the car
of bondage draw.
Here, here ! again cried he aloud, ye
kingdoms in decay,
Buy now a girdle for your realms, and
hold them to your sway.
What hopeless thraldom for a world might
these strong bands secure ;
So potent to subdue the great, and crush
the rebel poor.
Ye Cæsars listen ere too late, for soon shall
all men hear
The final word to sell these chains to
some brave buyer here.

LAST VENDUE

Is there no Alexander now would grasp
the globe again,
Ere my reluctant arm descend, and you
lament in vain?
All going—going!—At the word the list-
less throng awoke,
And down irrevocably came the long im-
pending stroke!
But lo, the old corroded links, drawn
clanking up to sight,
Fell piecemeal at the blow to earth—no
more to re-unite!

Then burst one thundering peal of joy from
all the gathered host,
Till mountain shouted to the sea, and coast
replied to coast!
The wo-worn earth, so hopeful long, for
that ecstatic time,
Put on again her eden robes in every hap
py clime,
And down the sky a glorious Zone the na-
tions saw descend,
Expanding o'er remotest hills, where hu-
man homes extend,
Till firm, within its glittering verge it shut
the world's wide span,
And bound, by lasting CHRISTIAN LOVE,
the heart of man to man.

www.ingramcontent.com/pod-product-compliance
Lightning Source LLC
LaVergne TN
LVHW011235110826
845150LV00006B/1643

* 9 7 8 1 4 2 5 5 1 4 5 5 6 *